Junior NKIERE MAKOLONI

COMPUTER COURSE FOURTH YEAR SA

Junior NKIERE MAKOLONI

COMPUTER COURSE FOURTH YEAR SA

ScienciaScripts

Imprint

Cover image: www.ingimage.com

This book is a translation from the original published under ISBN 978-620-6-71815-4.

Publisher:
Sciencia Scripts
is a trademark of
Dodo Books Indian Ocean Ltd. and OmniScriptum S.R.L publishing group

120 High Road, East Finchley, London, N2 9ED, United Kingdom
Str. Armeneasca 28/1, office 1, Chisinau MD-2012, Republic of Moldova, Europe
Managing Directors: Ieva Konstantinova, Victoria Ursu
info@omniscriptum.com

Printed at: see last page
ISBN: 978-620-8-51719-9

Contents

PREFACE

The purpose of national education is the harmonious training of the Congolese person, a responsible citizen, useful to himself and to society, capable of promoting the development of the country and national culture (Framework Law n°86-005 of 22 /09/1986 on National Education). Schools must therefore train citizens who are productive, creative, cultured, conscientious, free and responsible, open to social, cultural, aesthetic, spiritual and republican values (Education Charter, CNS, 1992).

In the education system, IT is both the source of all the hopes and the cause of all the evils.

Hopes because the potential of these devices is truly immense, on several levels:

- you can do "everything" with a computer: fundamental learning, training exercises with self-assessment, modelling, experimentation, simulation, resources: databases, etc.
- in all subjects: french, mathematics, biology, technology, vocational subjects;
- at all levels: primary, secondary (collège, lycee), higher education, adult education, initial and continuing training.

There have been a number of problems since it was first introduced, including difficulties in training teachers and getting pupils to use it, and difficulties in acquiring and managing equipment, and in setting up and running facilities (premises, security, etc.).

We would like to thank the Ministere Provincial de l'EPST Haut-Uele and the Inspection Principale Provincial de Haut-Uele 2 for their involvement in the production of this book, which will be of use not only to the Province of Haut-Uele but also to all the schools in our country that offer the Secretariat-Administration option.

SUMMARY

The teaching of computing is the action, the way of transmitting and making the learners acquire knowledge linked to Information and Communication Technologies aiming at the transformation of the latter. By the end of the course, learners will have developed new behaviours in relation to the new information and communication technologies.

Teaching computer science also involves training the young learners of tomorrow's society to be able to use the various information and communication technologies to inform themselves and communicate throughout the world. This will be achieved through the teaching they receive in computer science.

For Secretariat-Administration finalists, the book is not only much more oriented towards the concepts seen in the previous classrooms, but also includes new concepts to prepare the finalist for professional life and university without any difficulties whatsoever in the field of computing.

In this book, we have focused on the previous concepts of graph construction, the use of statistical function forms, the use of word processing tools, updating the antivirus, sorting data on the basis of criteria and, above all, creating databases in Excel with the drop-down list.

We are convinced that by using this book correctly, the finalists will have no difficulty or worry in facing the computer science tests at the state exam. We wish you much courage.

This book, which we hope will be comprehensible, practical and clear for final-year students, is also a compendium for teachers who wish to deepen their knowledge of computer science. It conforms to the national curriculum for primary, secondary and technical education in the Democratic Republic of the Congo, and takes into account the great evolution of computer science in terms of hardware and software. This is why this book focuses on hardware and software invariants.

We look forward to receiving your comments, criticisms and suggestions for improving this book, and encourage every school to buy a copy.

GENERAL OBJECTIVE

By the end of the fourth year of the humanities, the learner will be able to conceive and understand text correctly .[1]

SPECIFIC OBJECTIVES

Anyone who has followed this course assiduously will be able to :

- Building graphs ;
- Using the forms of statistical functions ;
- Use word processing tools ;
- Updating the antivirus ;
- Sort data by criteria.

[1] Cumculum-Livrable-Secretariat Administration, DRC ,2016.

CHAPTER I

EXCEL CHART

1.1. CHANGING CHART OPTIONS

To modify a graph ;

Right-click on your **graph**, then select Select data. In the Legend field (Series), click on the series you want to **modify**. Click on **Modify**, make the desired changes, then click on OK.

Or

a) Right-click on your graph, then **select Select data.**

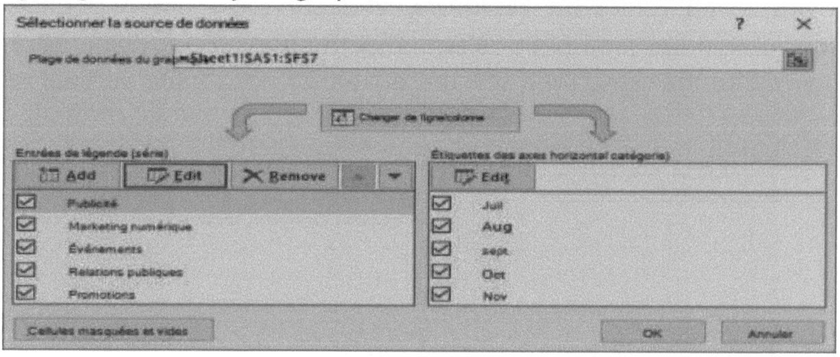

b) In the **Legend entry (Series)** area, click on the series you want to modify.

c) Click **Modify**, make the changes you want, then click **OK**.

NB: The changes you make may interrupt the links with the data source on the worksheet.

d) To reorganise a series, select it, then click on Move.

towards the **Aou** Move towards the

A. AXIS TITLE

a) Adding axis titles

Select your chart, then access the Chart Design tab which appears. Click on the arrow for the drop-down menu **Add Chart Element** Move the cursor over **Axis Titles**. In the pop-up window, select "**Primary Horizontal or Primary Vertical** or both.

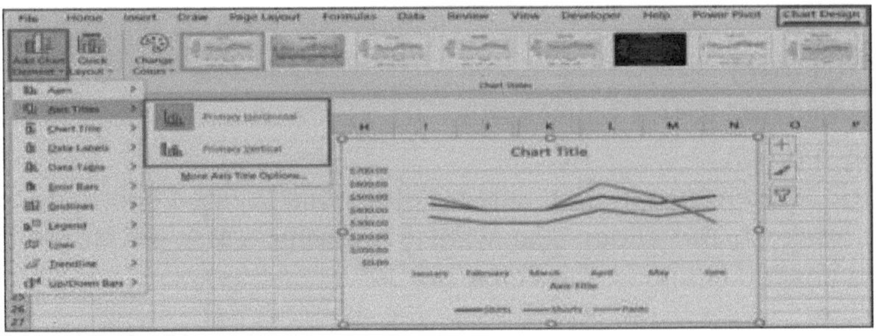

If you are using Excel on Windows, you can also use the chart elements icon to the right of the chart. Tick the box for axis titles, click on the arrow to the right, then tick the boxes for horizontal, vertical or both.

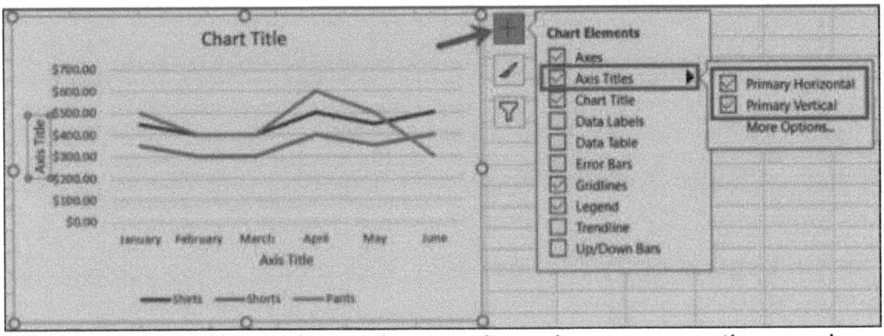

When the title of the axis you have selected appears on the graph,

it has a default name for the axis title. Select the text zone containing the default title and add your own.

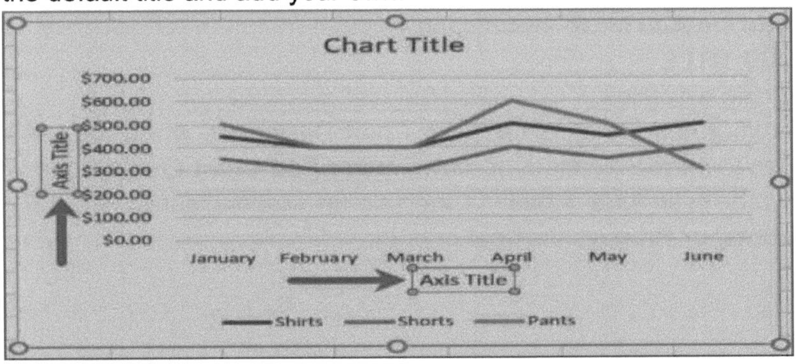

b) Customise the titles of the axes on the graph

You can customise both the axis title zones and the text inside these zones. And there are several ways of doing this.

First of all, right-click on the axis title to display the floating toolbar. You will see the Style, Fill and Outline options.

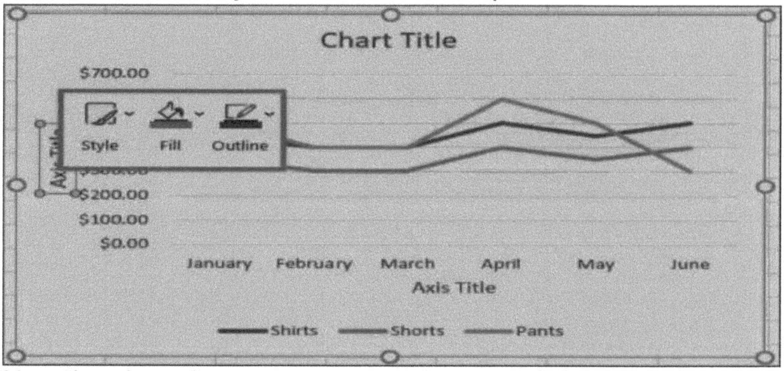

Use the drop-down arrows next to one of these options to apply a theme, use a gradient or texture, or choose a border style and colour.

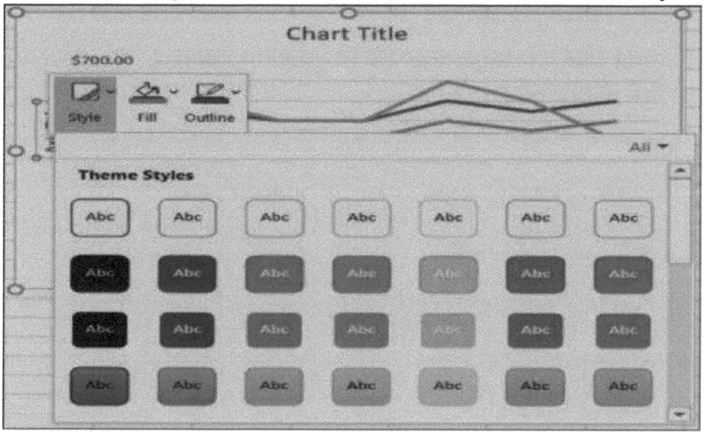

To increase customisation a little, start by opening the Format Axis Title sidebar. You can either right-click on an address and select "**Axis address format"**, or double-click on an address.

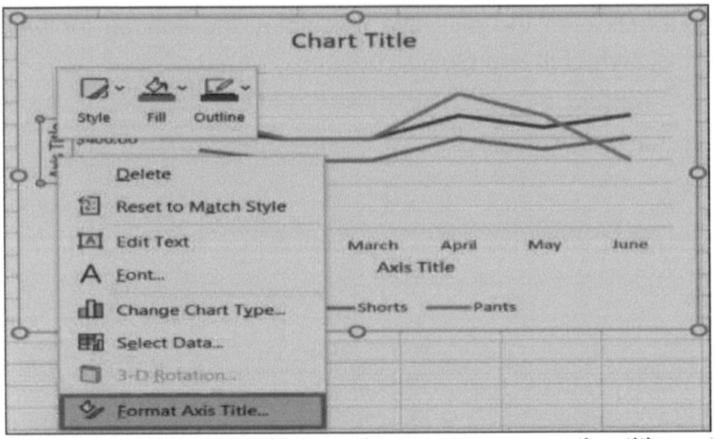

At the top of the sidebar, make sure you see the title options. Then use the three tabs just below for Fill & Line, Effects and Size & Properties to make your adjustments.

You can do things like change the fill or outline, add a shadow or glow, or adjust the alignment.

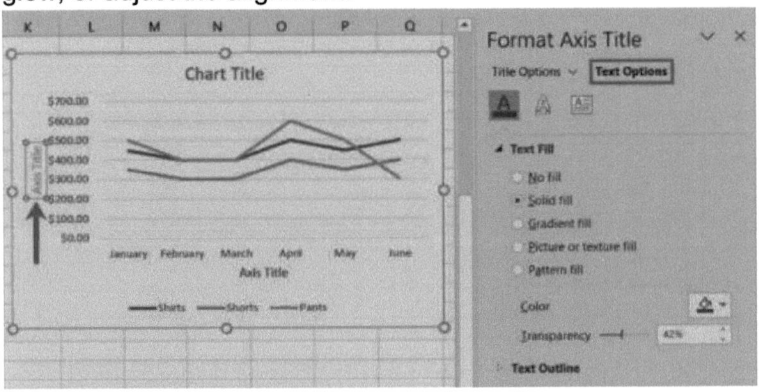

c) To customise the font

Select Text Options at the top of the sidebar. Then use the tabs for text fill, outline, text effects and text area.

You can then do things like change the colour or transparency of the font, use an XNUMXD format or change the direction of the text.

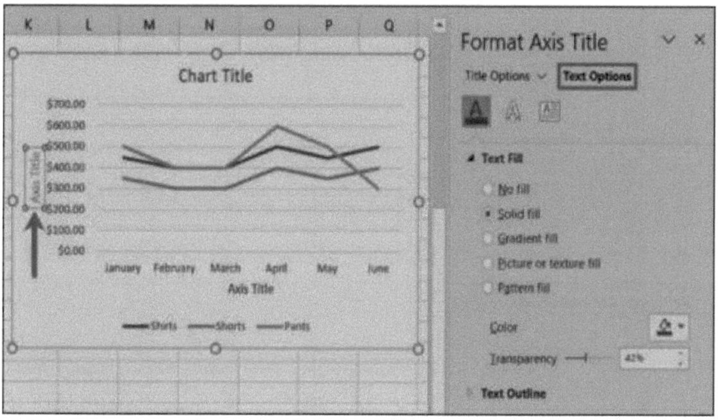

d) Delete chart axis titles

If you decide later to delete one or both of the axis titles, it will be just as easy to add them.

Select the chart and go to the Chart Design tab. Click on the down arrow Add Chart Element, move the cursor over the axis titles and deselect "Primary Horizontal", "Primary Vertical" or both.

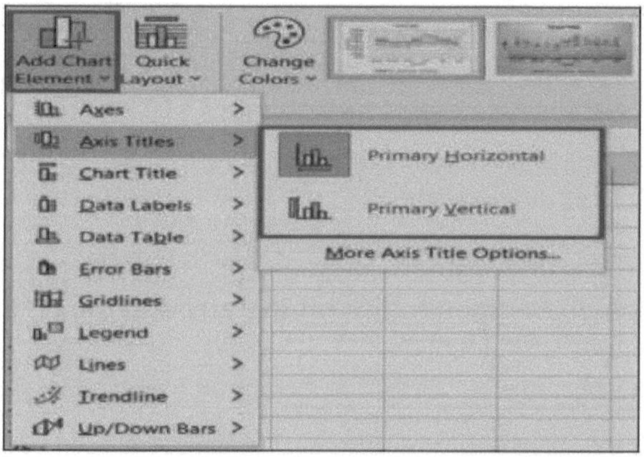

In Excel under Windows, you can also click on the chart elements icon and uncheck the axis titles box to delete both. If you want to keep a title, use the arrow next to the axis titles and select the one you want.

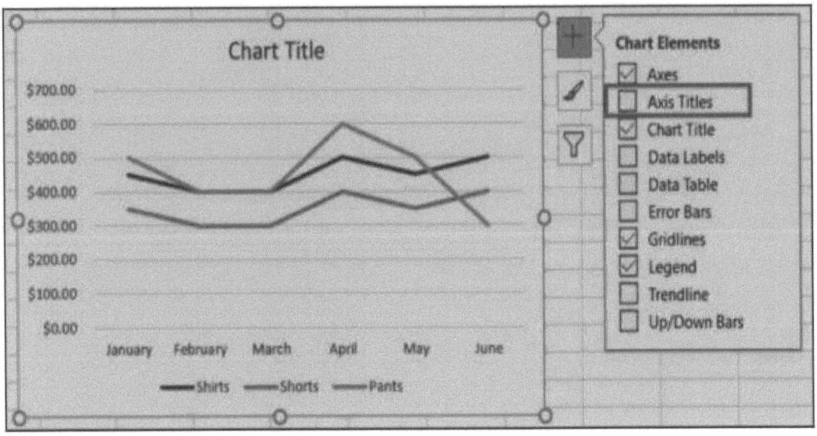

B. LEGEND

To legend a graph in Excel ;

1. **Click on the chart** to which you want to add a legend, click on the **Chart elements + button, then click on Legend.**

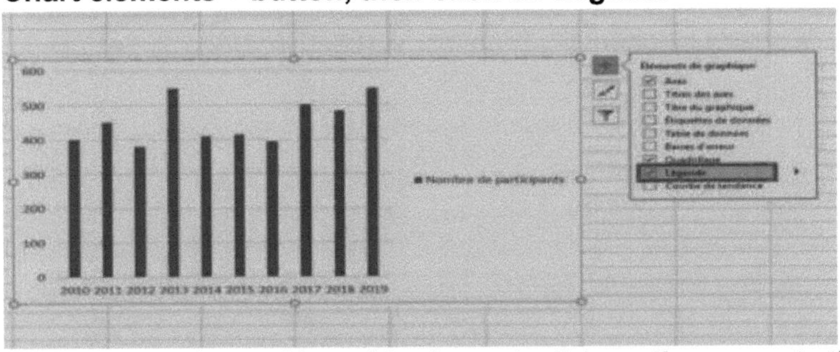

1. To change the position of the legend, click **on the arrow** to the right of legend, then select the desired location.

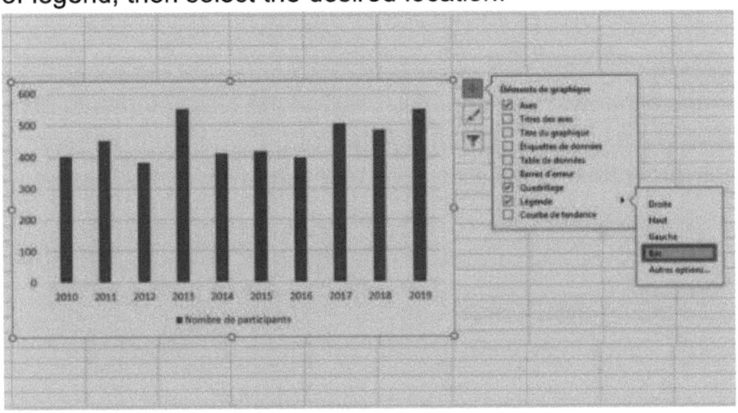

By default, a legend is not allowed to overlap a graphic. But if you're short of space, you can reduce the size of the graphic by clicking on **More options**, then unchecking **the Show legend without overlapping graphic** box.

To delete a caption, **right-click** on it, then click **Delete**.

C. DATA TABLES AND LABELS

1. DATA TABLE

Definition :

A data table is **a range of cells in which you can modify the values of certain cells and provide different answers to a problem**.

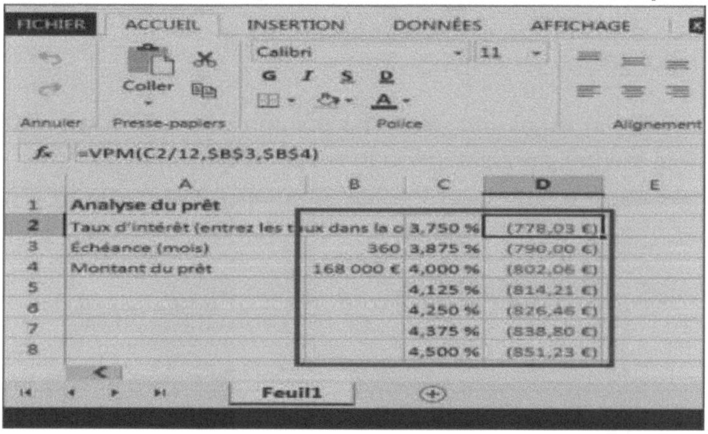

To create a data table, follow these steps:

Don't confuse data tables with Excel tables. A data table is a special range that Excel uses to calculate
several solutions to a formula.

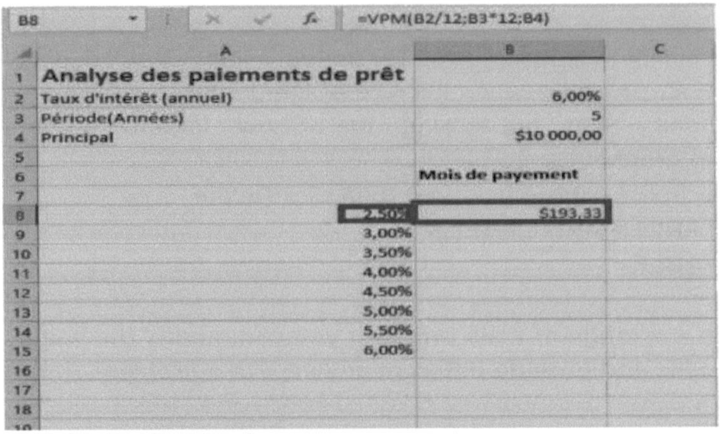

1) Enter the input values:

To type the values in a column, start the column one cell down and one to the left of the cell containing the formula, as shown here.
To type the values in a line, start the line one cell up and one to the right of the cell containing the formula.

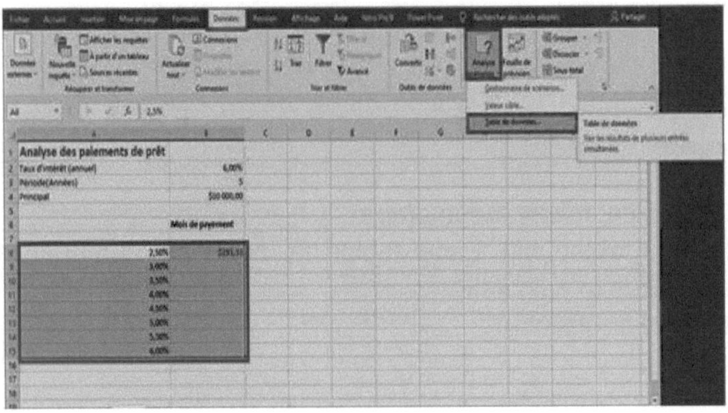

2) Select the range containing the input values and the formula.
3) Click on the Data tab.
4) Click on What-If Analysis.
5) Click on Data table.

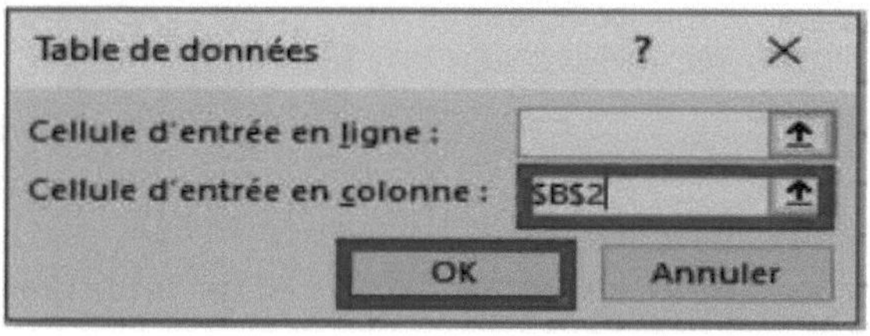

The Data Table dialog box is displayed.

6) Specify the formula cell you want to use as the input cell for the data table:

If the input values are in a column, enter the address of the input cell in the Input cell column text box.

If you have entered the input values in a row, enter the address of the input cell in the Row input cell text box.

7) Click OK.

2. DATA LABEL

To quickly identify a series of data in a graph, you can add data labels to the data points in the graph. By default, the data labels are linked to the values in the worksheet and update automatically when these values are changed.

Data labels make it easier to understand a graph, as they display details about a series of data or individual data points. For example, in the pie chart below, without the data labels, it is difficult to tell that coffee sales represent 38% of total sales. Depending on what you want to highlight in a graph, you can add labels to a series, to all the series (the whole graph) or to a data point.

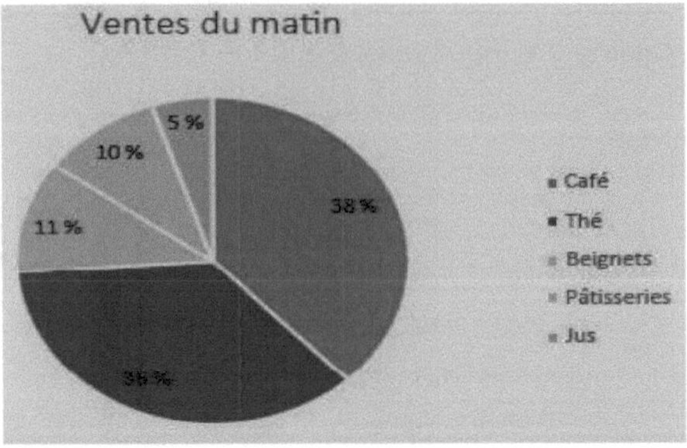

Note: The following procedures apply to Office 2013 and later versions.

Adding data labels to a graph

1. Click on the data series or graph. To add a label to a data point, after clicking on the series, click on the data point.
2. In the top right-hand corner, next to the graph, click on **Add a graphic element> data labels**.

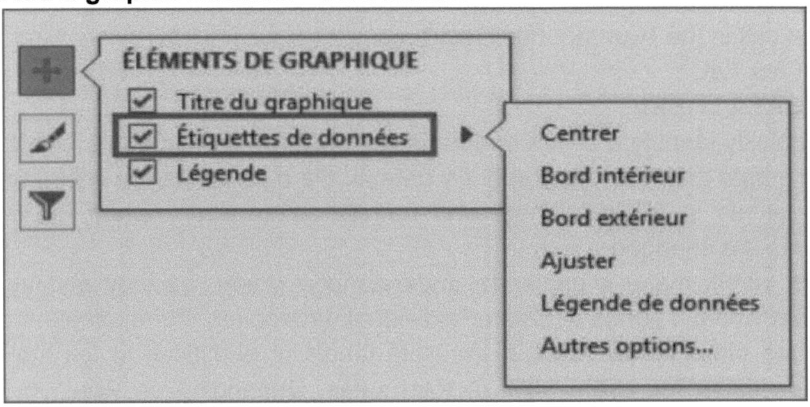

3. To change the location, click on the arrow and choose an option.
4. If you want to display the data label in a text bubble, click on **Data caption.**

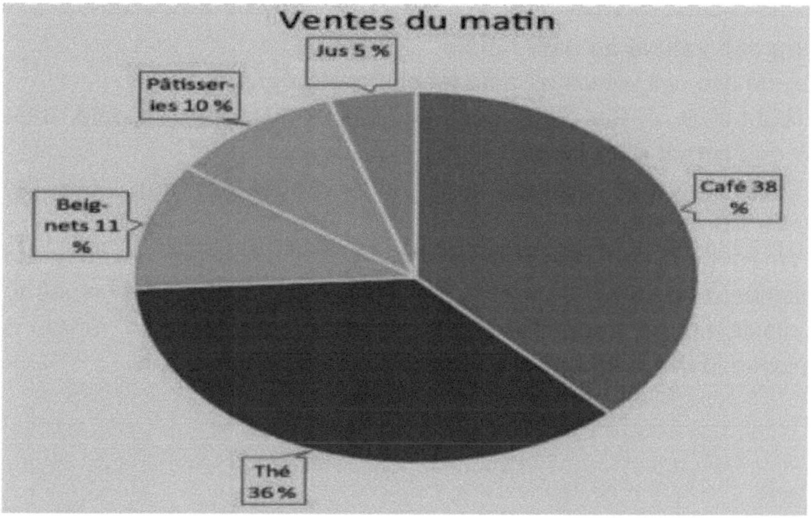

To make it easier to read the labels, you can move them inside the data points or outside the graph. To move a data label, drag it to the desired location.

If you decide that your labels are cluttering up your chart, you can delete them by clicking on them and pressing Delete.

NB: If the text in the data labels is not legible, resize the labels by clicking on them, then enlarging them to the desired size.

Changing the appearance of data labels

1. Right-click on the data series or label to display more data, then click **Format data labels**.
2. Click on **Label options** and under **Label content**, choose the options you want.

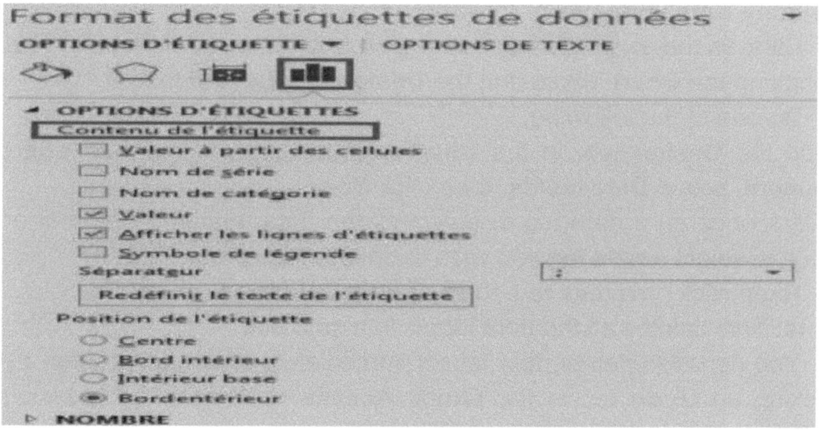

Using cell values as data labels

You can use cell values as data labels for your graph.

1. Right-click on the data series or label to display more data, then click on **Format data labels**.

2. Click on **Label options** and, under **Label contains**, tick the **Values from cells** box.

3. When the Data **Label Range** dialog box is displayed, return to the worksheet and select the range for which you want the cell values to be displayed as data labels. In this case, the selected range is displayed in the **Data Label Range** dialog box. Click on **OK**.

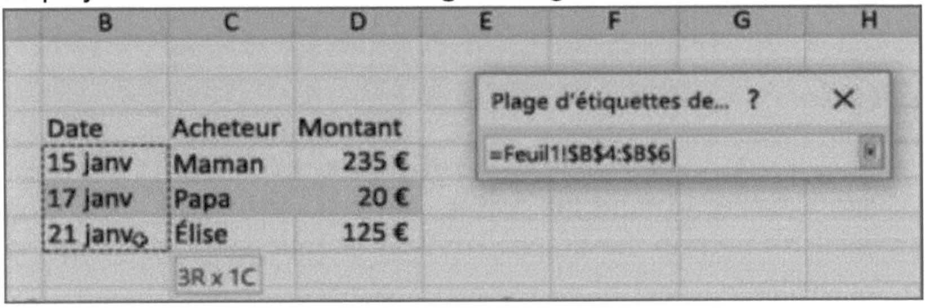

Cell values are now displayed as data labels in your graph.

Modifying the text of data labels

1. Click on the data label containing the text to be modified, then click on it again so that it is the only data label selected.

2. Select the existing text, then type the replacement text.

3. Click anywhere outside the data tag.

NB: If you want to add a comment to your graph or if you only have one data label, you can use a text box.

Deleting data labels from a graph

1. Click on the graph from which you wish to remove data labels. This brings up the **Chart Tools** and the **Design** and **Layout** tabs.

2. Do one of the following:

+ On the **Design** tab, in the **Chart layouts** group, click **Add chart element**, select **Data labels**, then click **None**.

+ Click once on a data tag to select all the data tags in a data set or twice to select a data tag you wish to delete, then press DELETE.

4- Right-click on a data tag, then click on **Delete**.

Note: This deletes all the data labels in a data set.

3. You can also delete data labels immediately after adding them by clicking on **Undo** EE in the **Quick Access toolbar** or by pressing

Ctrl+Z.

D. ARRIERE-PLANS

In Microsoft Excel, you can use an image as a sheet background for display purposes only. A sheet background is not printed and is not stored in an individual worksheet or in an element that you save as a web page.

Define the background of the Excel spreadsheet

You can add visual interest to a spreadsheet by replacing the background of the standard white sheet with a photo, drawing or other image.

For example, a spreadsheet tracking the amount needed for a future holiday might display a photo of the proposed destination as a back-plan.

When you choose the image you want to use as your background, make sure you select an image that won't make the spreadsheet text difficult to read. For example, if the text in your spreadsheet is dark, choose a light-coloured image as the background.

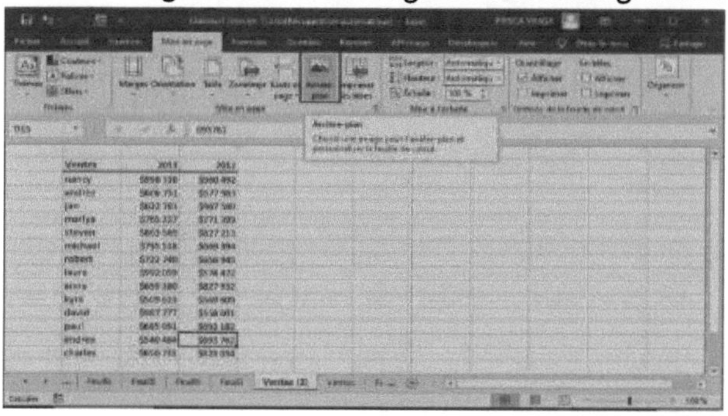

1) Click on the tab of the worksheet you want to customise;
2) Click on the Page Setup tab;
3) Click on Background.

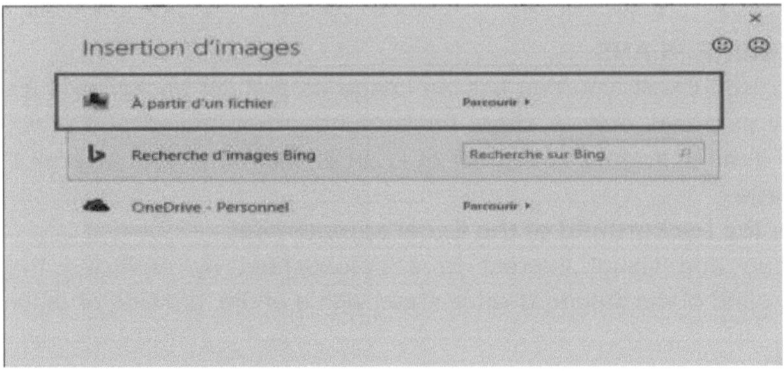

The Insert images dialogue box appears.

4) Click From a file.

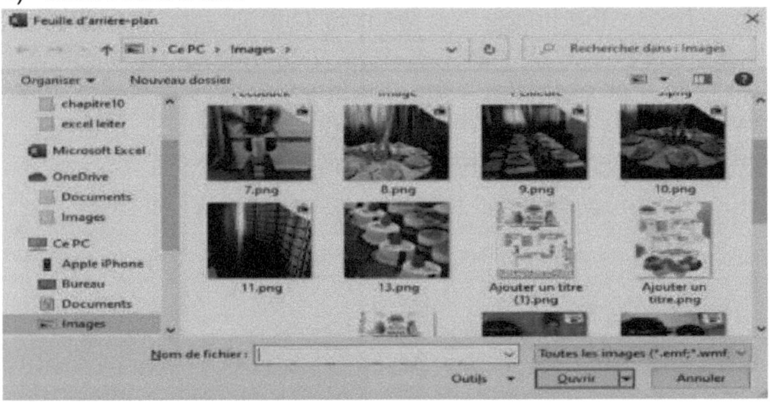

The Amere-plan sheet dialogue box appears.

5) Select the location of the image you want to use.
6) Click on the image.
7) Click on Insert.

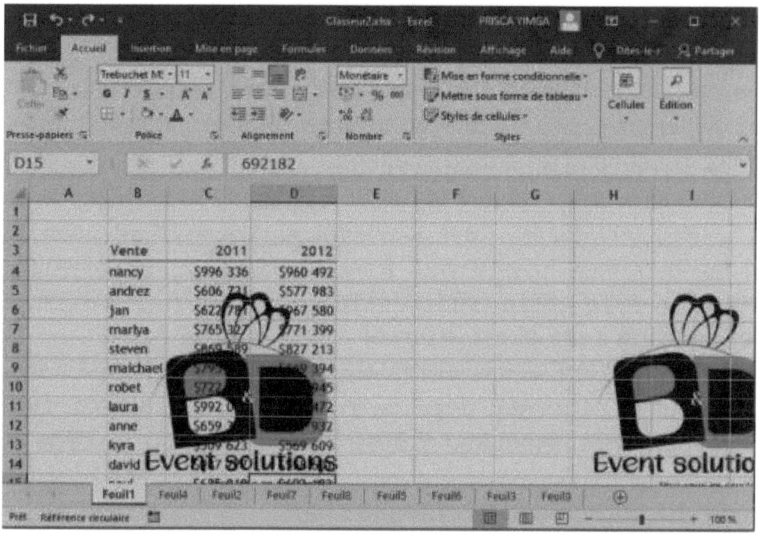

Excel formats the background of the worksheet with the image you have selected.

Applying a background colour instead of a background image

Excel does not have a command that changes the background colour of the entire worksheet.

Instead, you must first ;

1) select all the cells in the worksheet by clicking on Select all.

2) Click on the Home tab, on the arrow in the Fill colour drop-down list, then on the colour you want to use.

3) Excel applies the colour to the background of each cell.

Deleting the background image from the worksheet

If you find that having the background image makes it difficult to read the spreadsheet text, you should remove the background.

1) Click on the worksheet tab,

2) click on Page Setup and then click on Delete Background.

Excel deletes the background image from the worksheet.

E. SECTORS

Creating pie charts in Excel

Pie charts or pie graphs, as they are also known, are a common way of showing how much individual amounts or percentages contribute to the total. In such charts, the whole pie represents 100% of the whole, while the *slices of pie* represent portions of the whole.

People love pie charts, visualisation experts hate them, and the main scientific reason is that the human eye is unable to compare angles accurately.

But if we can't stop making pie charts, why don't we learn to do it properly? A pie chart can be difficult to draw by hand, with the tricky percentages presenting an added challenge.

However, in Microsoft Excel you can create a pie chart in a minute or two. And then, you might want to invest a few extra minutes in customising the charts to give your Excel pie chart a professionally crafted look.

Steps for creating a pie chart in Excel

Creating a pie chart in Excel is extremely simple and takes just a few clicks of a button. The key point is to organise the source data correctly in your spreadsheet and choose the most appropriate type of pie chart.

1) Prepare the source data for the pie chart.

Unlike other graphs, pie charts require the source data to be organised in a column or row. In fact, only one series of data can be plotted in a pie chart.

You can also include a column or row with category names, which must be the first column or row in the selection. The category names will appear in the pie chart legend and/or data labels.

In general, here are some of the characteristics of a pie chart:

- Only one set of data is plotted in the graph.
- All data values are greater than zero.
- There are no empty rows or columns.
- There should be no more than 7 to 9 data categories, as too many sectors can clutter up your graph and make it difficult to understand.

We are going to create a pie chart using the following data:

	A	B	C
1	Fruits	Pourcentages	
2	Ananas	36%	
3	Orange	14%	
4	Citron	13%	
5	Raison	28%	
6	Pomme	9%	
7			

2) Insert a pie chart in the current worksheet.

Once you have organised your source data correctly, select it, access the *Insert* tab and choose the type of chart you want. In this example, we create the most common 2D pie chart:

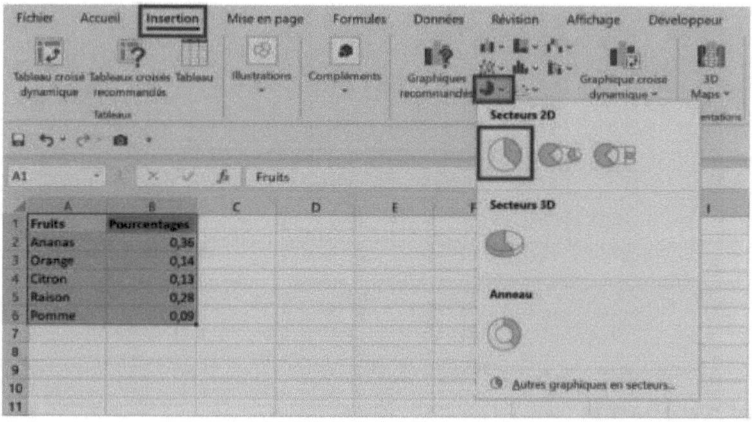

Include column or row headings in the selection if you want the column/value row heading to appear automatically in the title of your pie chart.

3) Choose the pie chart style (optional).

Once the new pie chart is inserted into your worksheet, you can go to the *Chart Creation* tab / *Charts* group and try out different pie chart styles to choose the one that best suits your data.

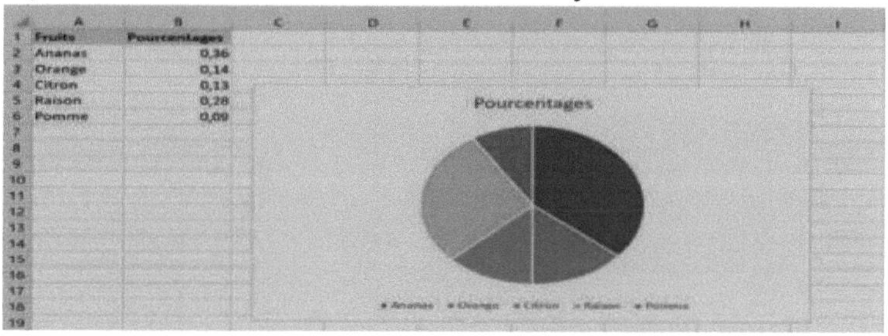

Creating different types of pie charts in Excel

When you create a pie chart in Excel, you can choose one of the following subtypes:

- 2D pie chart
- 3D pie chart
- Tarte a tarte or Barre de tarte
- Ring graph

2D Excel pie charts

This is the standard and most popular Excel pie chart that you would probably use most often. It is created by clicking on the 2D pie chart icon in the *Insert* tab / **Charts** group.

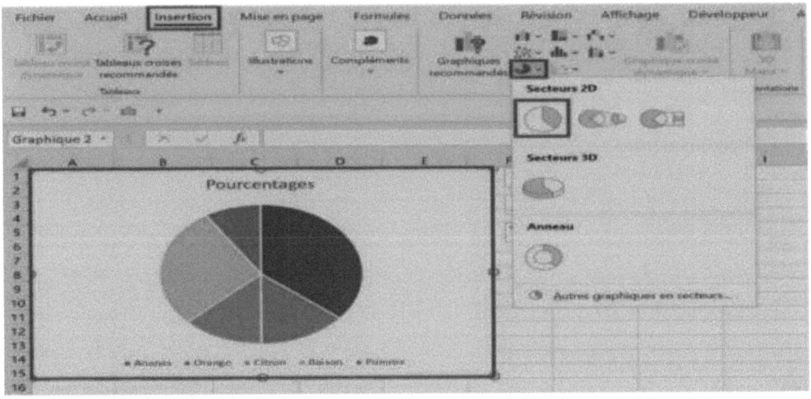

3D Excel pie charts

A 3D pie chart is similar to a 2D pie chart, but it displays the data on a third *axis.*
depth (perspective).

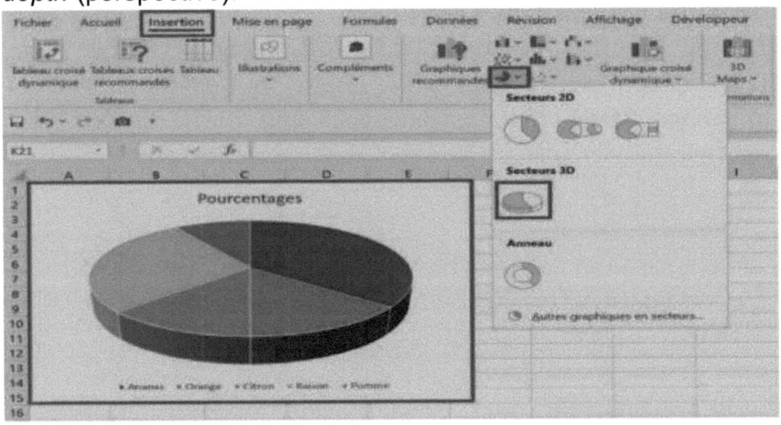

When you create 3D pie charts in Excel, you have access to additional features such as 3D rotation and perspective.

Bar and pie charts

If your Excel pie chart has too many small slices, you may want to create a pie chart and display small slices on an additional pie, which is a slice of the main pie.

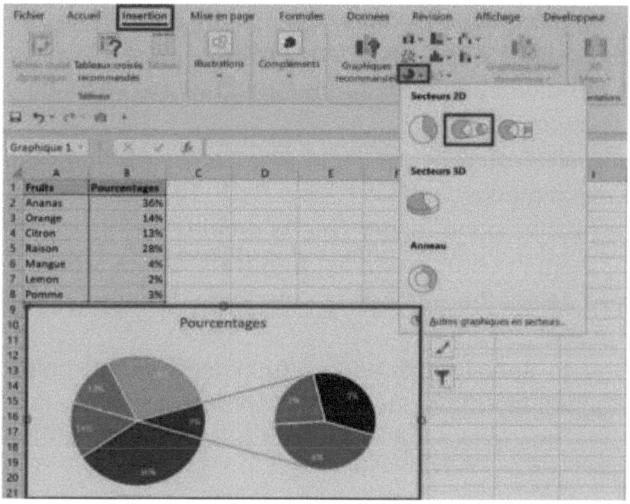

The sector bar chart is very similar to the sector chart, except that the selected slices are displayed on a secondary bar chart.

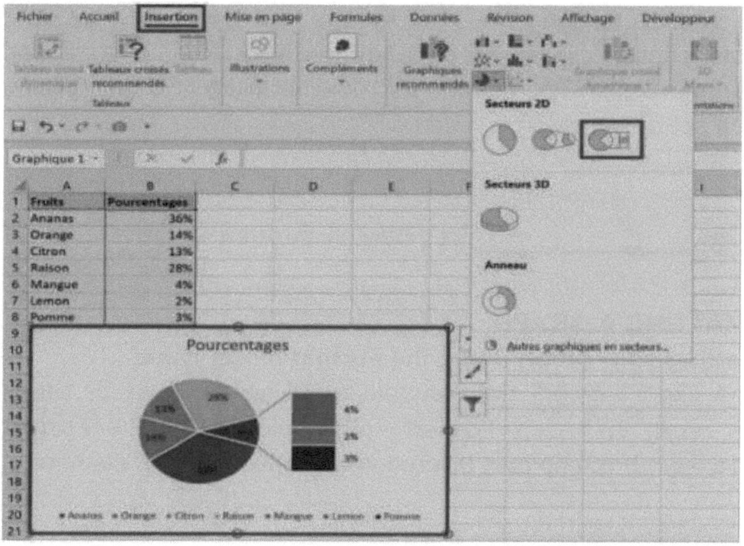

When you create a bar chart of sectors in Excel, the last 3 categories of data are moved to the second chart by default (even if they are the largest categories!). And because the default choice doesn't always work well, you can either :

. Sort the source data in your spreadsheet in descending order so that the worst-performing elements are included in the secondary graph, or

- Select the data categories to be moved to the second graph.

Choice of data categories for the secondary graph

To manually select the data categories to be moved to the secondary graph, proceed as follows:

1. Right-click on any slice of your pie chart and select *Format data series...* from the context menu.
2. In the *Layout data series* pane, under *Series options*, select one of the following options from the drop-down list **Separate series from**:

- *Position* - lets you select the number of categories to move to the second graph.
- *Value*- allows you to specify a threshold (minimum value) below which the data categories are moved to the additional graph.
- *Percentage value* - this is like the value, but here you specify the percentage threshold.
- *Custom* - allows you to manually select any slice of the pie chart in your spreadsheet, then specify whether you want to place it in the main or secondary chart.

In most cases, defining the percentage threshold is the most reasonable choice, but it all depends on your source data and personal preferences. The following screenshot illustrates the splitting of the data set by *percentage value*:

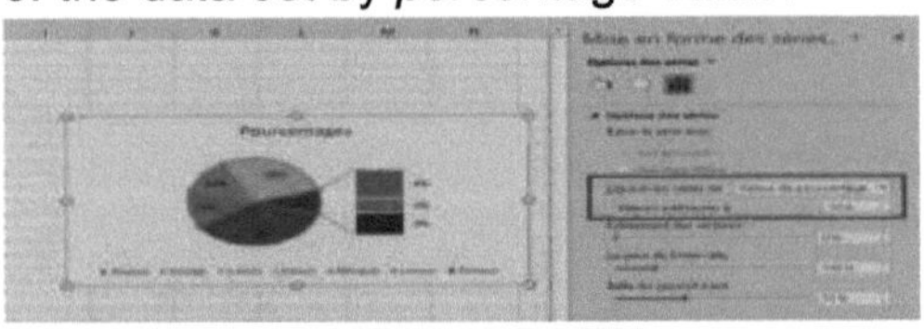

I.2.FORMATTING A GRAPH

A. Formatting your graph using the Format blobs panel

Select the chart element (for example, data series, axes or titles), right-click on it, then click **Format <chart element>**. The **Format** pane is displayed with options tailored to the selected chart element.

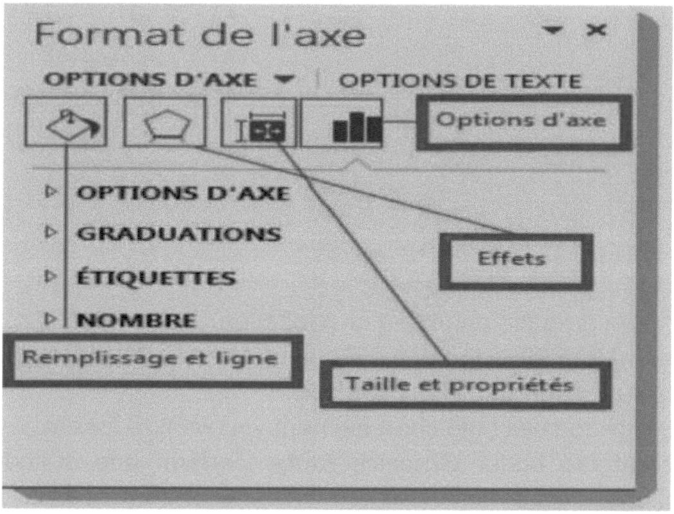

Clicking on the small icons at the top of the pane takes you to other parts of the pane with more options. If you click on another chart element, you'll see that the Office pane automatically updates to the new chart element.

For example, to format an axis :

1. Right-click on the graph axis, then click **Format axis**.

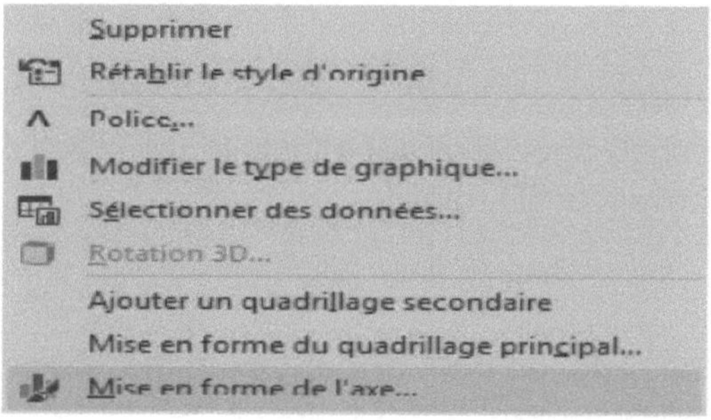

2. In the Office pane **Axis format** , make the following changes desired.

You can move or resize the Office pane to make it easier to use. Click on the chevron in the top right-hand corner.

○ Select **Move**, then drag the pane to a new location.

○ Select **Size**, then drag the edge of the pane to resize it.

B. Formatting your graph using the Ribbon

1. In your chart, click to select the chart element you want to format.

2. On the **Format** tab under Graphics **tools**, perform one of the following operations:

○ Click on **Shape fill** to apply a different fill colour, or a gradient, image or texture to the graphical element.

○ Click on **Shape outline** to change the colour, weight or size of the shape.
style of the graphic element.

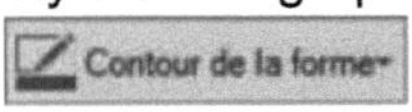

○ Click on **Shape effects** to apply special visual effects to the graphic element, such as shadows, bevels or 3D rotation.

○ To apply a predefined shape style, on the **Format** tab, in the **Shape styles** group, click on the style you want. To display all the available shape styles, click on the **Plus** 0 button.

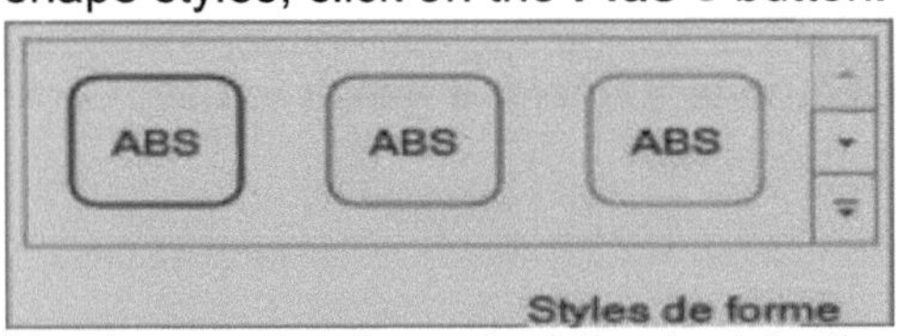

To change the format of the text in the graphic, select the text, then choose an option from the mini-toolbar which appears. Or, on the **Home** tab, in the **Font** group, select the formatting you wish to use.

To use WordArt styles to format text, select the text, then, in the **Format** tab of the **WordArt Styles** group, choose a WordArt style to apply. To display all the available styles, click on the **More** button.

CHAPTER II

CREATING A DATABASE

You are probably used to using Excel for tasks such as preparing reports or drawing up forecasts or budgets. However, when your needs do not justify the use of a full-fledged database management system (DBMS), Microsoft's spreadsheet software can also be used to create databases quickly. Excel's features enable you to manage your simple collections and query them efficiently.

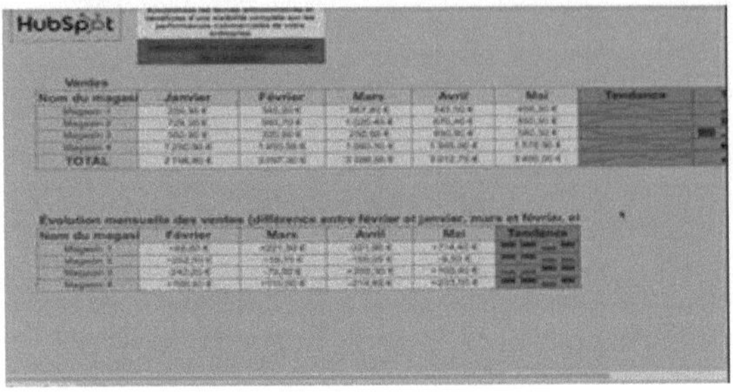

II.1. CREATING A DATABASE IN EXCEL

It takes just a few simple steps to create an Excel database in which to manage a collection of data. Once your records have been created, you can easily sort and filter your collection, update and reorganise it as required, and use Excel's powerful database functions to submit complex queries and calculations.

Defining your column headings in a new workbook

To begin, open a new workbook and define your column headings on line 1 of the **Sheet1** tab, taking into account the different types of information you feel are relevant to your collection.

In this example of a collection of flats under rental management for which an estate agent has been given responsibility by his branch manager, each line corresponds to a property sheet. The column headings are defined on the basis of the information that the agent considers relevant for each property, so that he knows quickly what he can offer for rent among the properties he manages when requests are made.

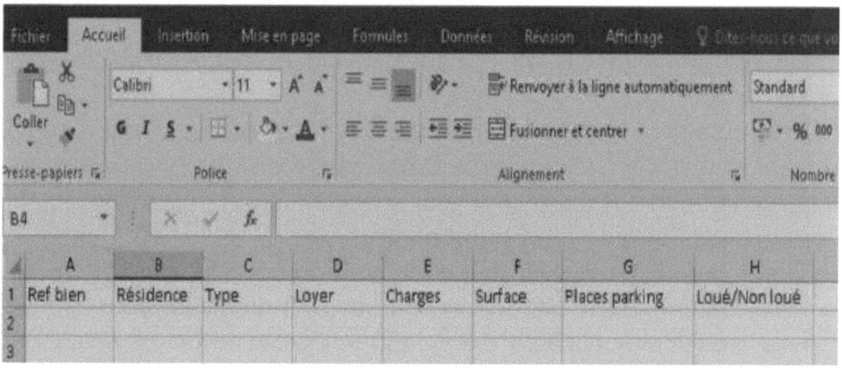

Click on cell **A1** and enter your first column heading. Click in the next cell, then enter the second, and so on until all your headings are defined.

Transforming your sheet into a database table

Note that at this stage, for Excel, your row 1 is nothing more than an ordinary row of data. For Excel to consider it as the row defining the fields in your database, declare it as the header row of a table.

To do this, select the cells containing your headings, and only those cells, then in the **Insert** tab, choose **Table.**

In the **Create a table** dialogue box, tick the **My table contains headers** box so that Excel understands that row 1 defines the fields in your database. Otherwise, it will switch the data in row 1 to row 2 and automatically create a row of Column1, Column2, Column3 headings, etc.

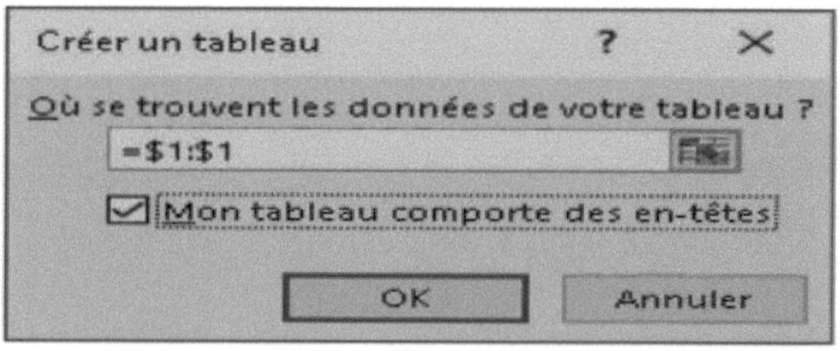

Click **OK** to confirm. The headings you specified in line 1 are now recognised by Excel as fields in your database, and are flanked by a drop-down list icon which will be useful later for sorting and filtering your data.

Note that the **Set as table** command, discussed below, allows you to obtain the same result, while also applying a specific style to your table.
Then double-click on **Sheet1**, at the bottom of the sheet, and rename the tab as you wish, for example **Database**, then save your database under a name that is explicit for your collection.

Configuring fields to limit input errors

To limit input errors in your database, you can create validation rules for cell content. Excel will then check in real time that your entries comply with the applicable rules, and will inform you of any input errors it detects.
For example, you can use such validation rules to restrict input to items in a given list, prohibit the input of numbers, dates or times outside a given range of values, or limit the length of text entered. You can even use a formula to check the validity of an entry, taking into account the value of other cells.
To apply a validation rule to a column, select the column, then in the **Data** tab, under **Data validation**, choose **Data validation**. In this example, the agent has chosen not to allow any value other than T2, T3, T4 or T5 to be entered in the **Type** field, as he currently has no other property types in his portfolio.

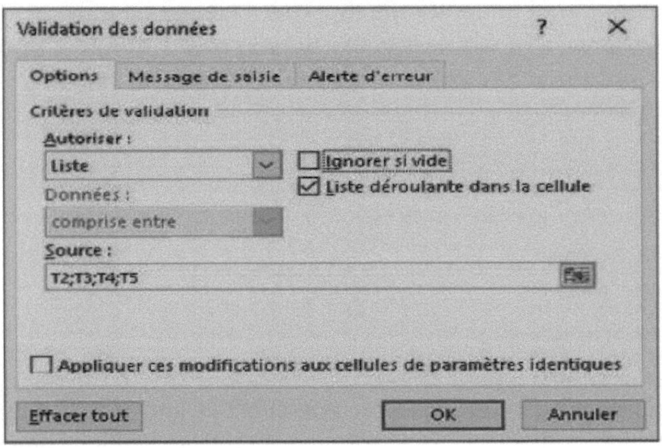

You can set up an alert message in the event of an input error. To do this, in the same window, open the **Error Alert** tab and specify the message that will be displayed if an error occurs. Under **Style**, you can make the validation rule prevent any entry other than a valid value by choosing **Stop**.

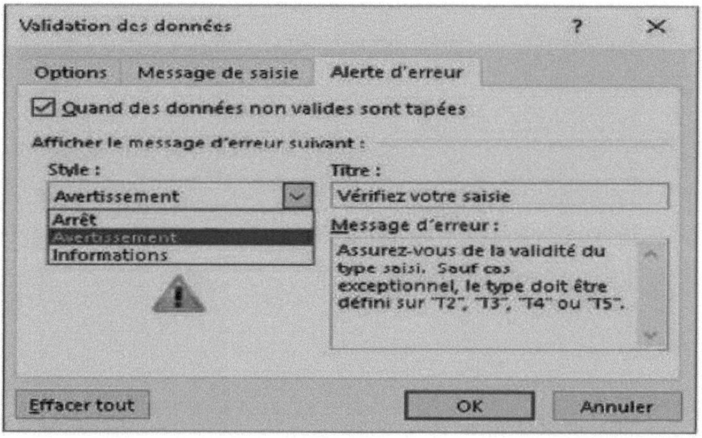

Confirm your rule by clicking **OK**.

In this example, only a warning message will be displayed in the event of an input error in the **Type** field, although this will not ultimately prevent the value detected as invalid from being entered if the user confirms it.

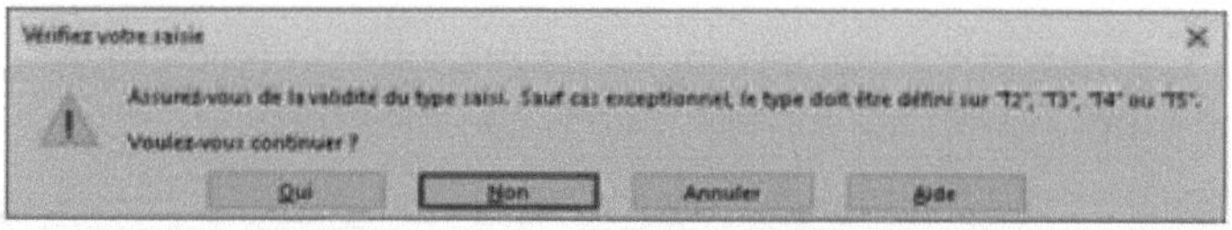

In the same way, configure validation rules for each field to which you wish to apply an input control, ensuring in each case that the rule is appropriate to the nature of the information.

Creation of a form to speed up data entry

Once you have defined your database fields and validation rules, you can log your records in "classic" mode, by filling in the different cells in each row of data, one row at a time.

When there are many fields and a large number of records, it can nevertheless become tedious to fill in the database in this way. To make data entry quicker and easier, you can use an input mask to create a form.

To make the **Form** function available on the Ribbon, under **File**, choose **Options**, then in the **Excel Options** dialogue box, click **Customise Ribbon**.

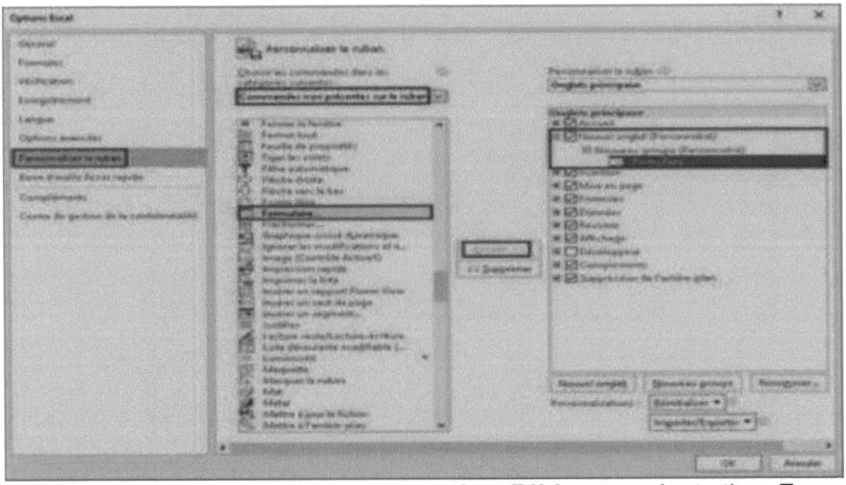

Choose the **Commands not on the Ribbon**, select the **Form** command, then add it to a **New Group** under a **New Tab**.

To define your input mask, select the cells defining the fields in your database, and only those cells, then in your **New Tab** on the Ribbon, click **Form.**

The form that appears automatically includes the various fields in your database in an input mask that makes it easy to enter data.

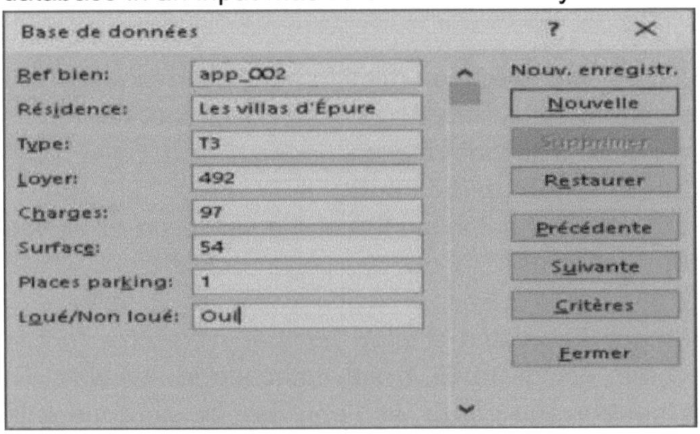

Once you have filled in the fields for your first record, click **New** to validate it. The record is automatically inserted into your database table, with the delimitation zone extending downwards accordingly.

Enter your next records in the same way. **The Next** and **Previous** buttons on the form allow you to navigate through your records, modifying or deleting them as required. When you have finished, click

Close.

In your table, the drop-down icons associated with the field names allow you to sort and filter your records.

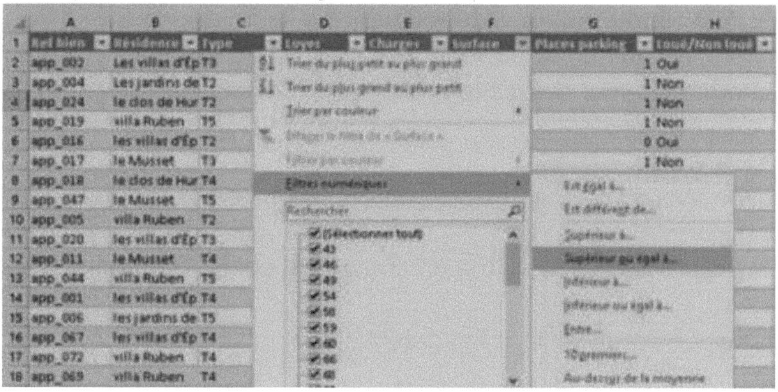

Here, for example, the numeric filter **Greater than or equal to** applied to the **Surface area** field will produce a list of all flats with a surface area greater than or equal to a given number of square metres. And by combining this filter with a second, applied to the "Rented/Not rented" field and set to **Yes**, the agent will be able to know which of these flats he can offer for rent.

This means you can combine several filters, applied to different fields, to isolate precisely the information you need.

Formatting data

If you want to change the default formatting applied to your database table, click in any cell of the table, then in the **Home** tab, click **Set as table.**

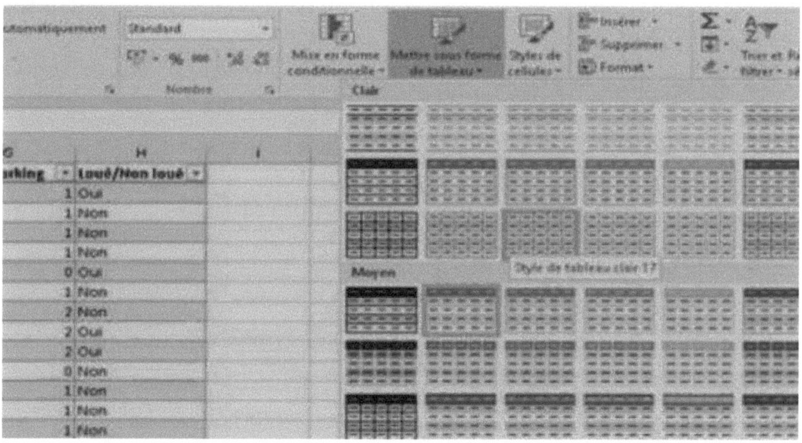

Hover over the different styles to preview how they will look in your table, then click on the one you want to apply.

Useful Excel functions for a database

Excel offers a number of powerful database functions that you can use to interrogate your database and perform calculations on samples of data.

BDMOYENNE

Returns the average of the selected database entries.

BDNB

Counts the number of cells in the database that contain numbers.

BDNBVAL

Counts the non-empty cells in the database.

BDLIRE

Extract from the database a single record meeting the criteria.

BDMAX

Returns the maximum value of the selected database entries.

BDMIN

Returns the minimum value of the database entries selected.

BDPRODUIT

Multiplies the values of a particular field in the database records which meet the specified criteria.

BDECARTYPE

Calculates the standard deviation for a sample of selected database entries.

BDECARTYPEP

Calculates the standard deviation for an entire population of selected database entries.

BDSOMME

Adds the numbers in the field column of the database records that meet the criteria.

BDVAR

Calculates the variance for a basic input sample of

CHAPTER III

STATISTICS FUNCTION

111.1. DEFINITION

Statistical functions are **used to perform statistical analyses on numbers** (and on dates and times in the case of certain functions).

111.2. MINIMUM FUNCTION

What is the purpose of the MIN function in Excel?

Excel's MIN function **displays the smallest value in a given selection**.

Identifying a minimum in Excel can be useful for compiling statistics or simply highlighting the youngest age in a group, the lowest mark in an exam or the lowest monthly turnover in a given year or region. The MIN option on Excel makes your data easier to read and analyse.

Syntax of the MIN function in Excel

To identify the minimum in Excel, apply the **=MIN(range_of_values)** function if you are looking for a minimum number in a range of cells, or **=MIN(value_1; value_2; value_3; etc.)** if you are looking for a list of values.

The arguments of MIN on Excel can be :

. numbers ;

. names ;

- matrices ;
- references containing numbers.

Note that empty cells are not taken into account, nor are logical values or text included in the matrix or reference. Only the numbers and error values of these elements are considered when using a MIN Excel formula. Furthermore, if the arguments entered cannot be converted into numbers, the spreadsheet will display an error. Also, the value 0 is generated automatically when the arguments do not contain any numbers.

Example of use of the MIN function

Let's look at a table showing a company's sales figures for each city in which it is based over a number of years. If you want to **see the lowest turnover** in each city for all years, go to the cell of your choice and enter =MIN. The spreadsheet will suggest the function you are looking for, which you should double-click.

Then select the range containing all the annual sales figures for the first city, and close the parenthesis in Excel's MIN formula before pressing the "Enter" key. The figure displayed is therefore the **lowest**

turnover achieved in the first city, whatever the year.

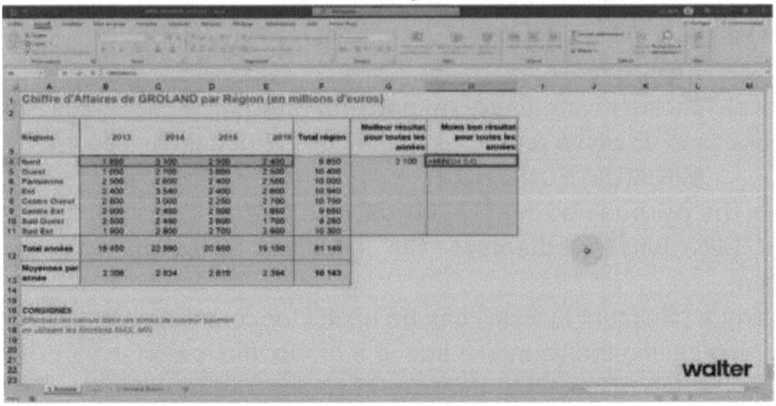

To extend the MIN function to other cities without repeating the operation, use incremental copying. This will give you the lowest value for each city at a glance.

111.3. MAXIMUM FUNCTION

When should you use the MAX function in Excel?

Excel's MAX formula is used to **identify the largest number** in a series of values. So, if you need to know which element in your database contains the highest score or the highest mark, this is the formula to use. It's very popular because it saves you a lot of time.

Consequently, learning Excel requires knowledge of this function. It can also be useful for producing statistics and identifying the frequency with which a given maximum value appears in a given region of the world, for example.

Syntax of the MAX function in Excel

To apply MAX correctly to Excel, you need to know its syntax, which is as follows:

. **=MAX(range_of_values)** if you are looking for a maximum value in a range of cells ;

. **=MAX(value_1; value_2; value_3; etc.)** if your search is for a list of values.

The arguments to be inserted into your MAX Excel formula can be names, matrices, numbers or references that contain numbers. If you add a matrix or a reference, note that only the error values of these, as well as the numbers, are taken into account.

You can also enter logical values and textual representations of numbers directly in the list of your arguments; they will be taken into account. On the other hand, empty cells, logical values or text contained in the matrix or reference will be ignored. Similarly, **if the arguments to Excel's MAX function do not contain any numbers, the spreadsheet returns 0**. Finally, if the spreadsheet cannot convert arguments in the form of error values or text into numbers, you will get an error.

Example of use of the MAX function

If you want to **identify the best mark obtained** in a class, go to the cell where the result is to be collected. Type =MAX then double-click on the suggestion in the spreadsheet. Then select the range containing your marks using your mouse, close the parenthesis and confirm with the "Enter" key.

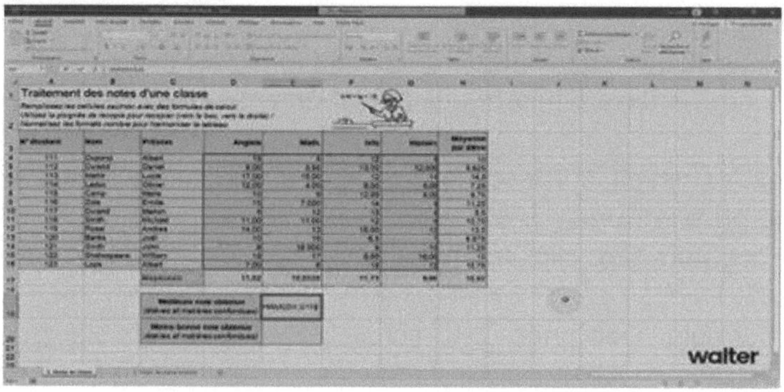

The entire range has been scanned by the spreadsheet and the figure generated by using MAX on Excel corresponds to the maximum mark obtained in your class.

111.4. AVERAGE

A. Calculating a simple average

1. Select cells A2 to A7 (values in the Quality column of the l'unite).

2. In **the Formulas tab,** click on the arrow at for the function click on **Average.**

The result is 8.166666667.

B. Calculating the average for non-adjacent cells

1. Select the cell in which you want the average to appear, for example cell A8, which is the cell to the left of the cell containing the text "Average unit quality" in the example data.

2. Under **the Formulas tab,** click on the L?J arrow for the function

#x0, click on Average, then press Return.

3. Click on the cell containing the average you have just created (cell A8 in this example).

The formula is displayed in the formula bar, **=MOYENNE(A2:A7)** if you are using example data.

4. In the **formula bar,** select the content in brackets (**A2:A7** if you are using example data).

5. Hold down the , click on the cells you want to average, then press Return. For example, select A2, A4 and A7, then press Return.

Excel the range reference selected in the AVERAGE function with cell references for the cells you have selected. In this example, the result is 8.

C. Calculating a weighted average

This example calculates the average price paid for a unit for all orders, where each order is for a different number of units at a different price per unit.

1. Select cell A9, which is the cell to the left of the cell containing the text "Average price per unit".

2. On **the Formulas tab,** click **Insert** a function to open the **Formula Designer** pane.

3. In the Formula **Designer** list, scroll down and double-click **SOMMEPROD.**

Tip: To find a function quickly, click on **the** Search for a function box, then start typing the name of the function. For example, start typing **SOMMEPROD.**

4. Click on the box below **matrix1,** then in the sheet, select cells B2 to B7 (values in the Price per unit column).

5. Click on the box below **matrix2,** then in the sheet, select cells C2 to C7 (values in the column Number of units ordered).

6. In the formula bar, click to the right of the closing parenthesis in the formula, then type ***/*.**

If you do not see the formula bar, in **the** View menu, click **Formula** bar.

7. In the Formula **designer** list, double-click **SUM.**

8. Select the range in the **number1 area,** press DELETE, then in the sheet, select cells C2 to C7 (values in the Number of units column).

The formula bar should now contain the following formula: =SOMMEPROD(B2:B7;C2:C7)/SOMME(C2:C7).

9. Press RETURN.

This formula divides the total cost of all orders by the total number of units ordered, giving a weighted average per unit of 29.38297872.

D. Calculating an average that ignores specific values

You can create a formula which excludes specific values. In this example, you are going to create a formula to calculate the average unit quality of all units whose revaluation is greater than 5.

1. Select cell A10, which is the cell to the left of the cell containing the text "Average quality of all units with a score above 5".
2. On **the Formulas tab,** click **Insert** a function to open the **Formula Designer** pane.
3. In the Formula **designer** list, double-click on **AVERAGE.SI.**

Tip: To find a function quickly, click on **the** Search for a function box, then start typing the name of the function. For example, start typing **AVERAGE.IF.**

4. Click on the box next to the range, then, in the sheet, select cells A2 to A7 (values in the Price per unit column).
5. Click on the box next to **the criterion,** then type **" >5"**.
6. Press RETURN.

The formula excludes the value in cell A7 from this calculation and produces an average unit quality of 8.8.

Tip: To use the **AVERAGE.IF** function to calculate an average that excludes zero values in a list of numbers, type **"<>0"** in the field next to the **criterion**.

111.5.50 MME, STANDARD DEVIATION, VARIANCE

111.5.51 SOMME

The purpose of the SUM function in Excel is to add values. Using this function, you can :

- add individual values ;
- references ;
- cell ranges ;
- a combination of the three options.

Let's look at some examples of the Excel SUM formula:

- =SUM(A2:A9): this formula adds the values in cells A2 to A9 ;
- =SUM(A2: A9; C1:C8): this adds the values in cells A2:A9, as well as cells C1:C8.

The function :

Excel allows you to **calculate the sum of the values in a range** which meet the specified criterion. For example, in a column containing numbers, you only wanted to calculate the sum of values greater than 6. You could therefore use the following formula: =SUM.SI (B2:B25,">6").

In addition, **the SUM.SI.ENS Excel function adds together all its arguments**, the sum of all its arguments meeting several criteria.

1. Use the automatic sum

Thanks to the Excel SUM function, the software can perform mathematical operations for you:

- **add the sum of an Excel column** ;
- add a number line.

To do this, you need to select a cell next to the numbers you want to add together, then click on "Autosum" in the "Home" tab. Then press "Enter". Once you click on **Excel Autosum**, Excel will automatically insert a formula to add the numbers together.

Finally, press "Enter" to display the result in cell B7. You can also **display the Excel addition formula** in the dedicated bar at the top of the Excel window.

2. Adding several numbers in a cell

To add cells containing several numbers, you need to :

- click on an empty cell and type the equals sign (=) to start writing the formula;
- After the equals sign, type in some numbers, all separated by a plus sign (+) (for example, 30+20+10+2);
- Press "Back".

3. Summing numbers using cell references

A cell reference is the combination of the column letter and the row number (for example, A3 or D234). When you use cell references in a formula, instead of the cell value, you can change the value without changing the formula.

To do this:

1. Type a number in cell C1 and a number in cell D1.
2. Type an equals sign (=) in cell E1 to begin constructing the formula.
3. After the equals sign, type C1+D1.
4. Press "Back".

5. Quick total from a row or column

To perform a quick total from a row or column, you need to :

- type in some numbers in a column or row, then select the range of cells you have just filled in;
- Look at the value shown in the status bar next to "Sum".

III.5.2.GAP

By calculating the standard deviation, you can refine the result returned by an AVERAGE. Let's see how to use it in Excel

1. Interest of standard deviation

Let's take the case of a class of 10 pupils

. In the A exam, all the students scored 10; the average is obviously 10.

. For the B exam, 5 students scored 0 and 5 students scored 20. **The average is once again 10**

As you can imagine, the analysis that can be made is radically different between the two exams, **even though the average is the same.**

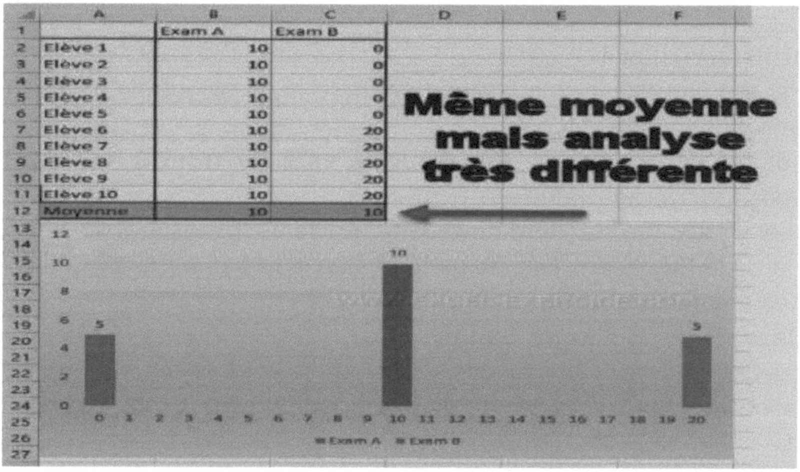

This is where calculating **the standard deviation** will help us to better **analyse our average.**

2. Calculating the standard deviation in Excel

The standard deviation is simply calculated using the function **ECARTYPE(Cell range)**.

Applied to our example, we find 0 for the first case and 10.54 for the second.

=ECARTYPE(B2:B11) => 0

=ECARTYPE(C2:C11) => 10,54

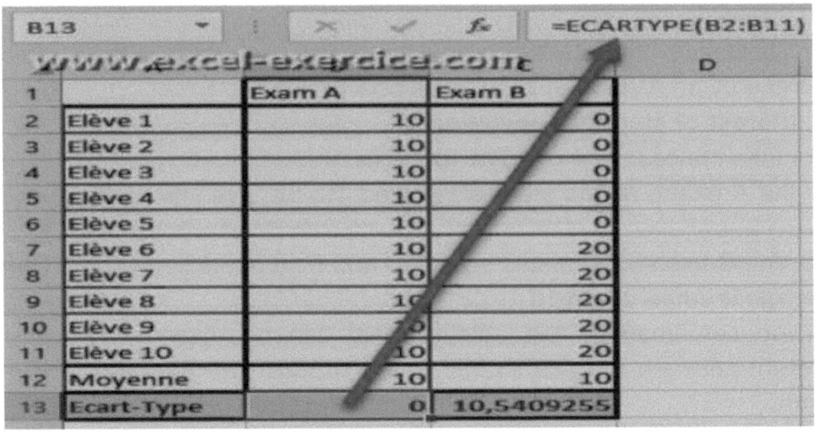
B13 =ECARTYPE(B2:B11)

	Exam A	Exam B
Elève 1	10	0
Elève 2	10	0
Elève 3	10	0
Elève 4	10	0
Elève 5	10	0
Elève 6	10	20
Elève 7	10	20
Elève 8	10	20
Elève 9	10	20
Elève 10	10	20
Moyenne	10	10
Ecart-Type	0	10,5409255

What do these results mean?

- For the first result, **0** indicates that there is no difference between my average and the values.
- For the second series, **the result is very far from 0** and even exceeds the average value.

In other words, the standard deviation represents the dispersion of the data around the mean. The closer the value is to 0, the more the data studied are centred on the mean.

3. Case study: Bollinger Bands

In chartist analysis - the analysis of stock market prices - standard deviation is used to determine buy and sell signals using Bollinger bands.

If the share price touches the moving average + 2 standard deviations, this means that the share price has risen too fast. It is therefore a sell signal.

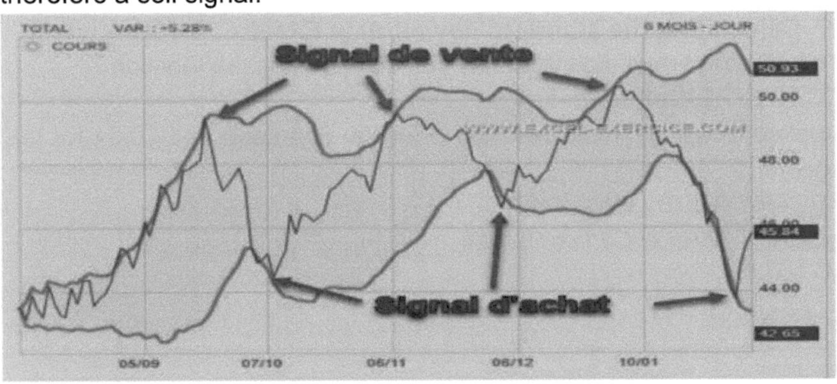

III.5.3.VARIANCE

Variance is a measure of the variability of a set of data, indicating the extent to which different values are distributed.

Mathematically, it is defined as the average of the deviations from the mean.

To better understand what you are actually calculating with variance, consider this simple example.

Suppose y 5 tigers in your local zoo who are 14, 10, 8, 6 and 2 years old.

To find the variance, follow these simple steps:

1. Calculate the average (simple average) of the five numbers:

$$Mean = \frac{14 + 10 + 8 + 6 + 2}{5} = 8$$

2. From each number, subtract the average to find the differences. To visualise this, plot the differences on the graph:

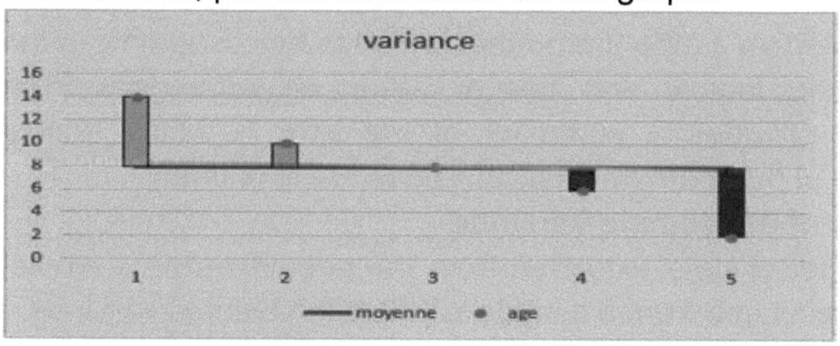

3. Check each difference.
4. Calculate the average of the squared differences.

$$Variance = \frac{6^2 + 2^2 + 0^2 + (-2)^2 + (-6)^2}{5} = 16$$

So the variance is 16. But what does this number really mean?

In reality, the variance only gives you a very general idea of the dispersion of the data set. A value of 0 means that there is no variability, in other words that all the numbers in the data set are identical. The larger the number, the more dispersed the data.

This example concerns the variance of the population (i.e. 5 tigers represent the entire group you are interested in). If your data is a selection from a larger population, you need to calculate the variance of the sample using a slightly different formula.

1. How to calculate variance in Excel

There are 6 built-in functions for calculating variance in Excel: VAR( ),

VAR.S( ), VARP( ), VAR.P( ), VARA( ) and VARPA( ).

Your choice of variance formula is determined by the following factors:

> The version of Excel you are using.
> The variance of the sample or population.
> You want to evaluate or ignore text and logical values.

The table below gives an overview of the variation functions available in Excel to help you choose the formula best suited to your needs.

Name	**Excel version**	**Data type**	**Text and logic**
VAR	2000 - 2019	Sample	Ignore
VAR.S	2010 - 2019	Sample	Ignore
VARA	2000 - 2019	Sample	Evaluates
VARPE	2000 - 2019	Population	Ignore
VAR.P	2010 - 2019	Population	Ignore
VARPA	2000 - 2019	Population	Evaluates

2. VAR.S( ) against VARA( ) and VAR.P( ) against VARPA( )

VARA( ) and VARPA( ) differ from other variance functions only in the way they handle logical and textual values in references. The following table provides a summary of the way in which textual representations of numbers and logical values are evaluated.

3. Calculation of the sample variance

A sample is a set of data extracted from the population as a whole. The variance calculated from a sample is called the sample variance.

For example, if you wanted to know how people's heights vary, it would be technically impossible to measure every single person on earth. The solution is to take a sample of the population, say 1,000 people, and estimate the size of the whole population based on that sample.

The variance of the sample is calculated using this formula:

$$Sample\ variance = \frac{\sum(x-\bar{x})^2}{(n-1)}$$

Or:

-k xis the mean (simple average) of the values in the sample.
-k **n** is the size of the sample, i.e. the number of values in the sample.

There are 3 functions for finding the sample variance in Excel: VAR( ), VAR.S( ) and VARA( ).

VAR( ) function in Excel

This is the oldest Excel function for estimating variance based on a sample. The VAR( ) function is available in all versions of Excel from 2000 to 2019.

= VAR(number1; [number2]; ...)

In Excel 2010, the VAR( ) function has been replaced by VAR.S( ), which offers improved precision. Although VAR( ) is still available for backwards compatibility, it is recommended that VAR.S( ) is used in current versions of Excel.

VAR.S( ) function in Excel

This is the modern equivalent of the Excel VAR( ) function. Use the VAR.S( ) function to find the sample variance in Excel 2010 and later versions.

= VAR.S(number1, [number2], ...)

A. VARA( ) function in Excel

The Excel function VARA( ) returns a variance sample based on a set of numbers, text and logical values, as shown in the table above.

B. = VARA(value1; [value2]; ...)

Example of a variance formula

When working with a set of numerical data, you can use one of the above functions to calculate the variance of the sample in Excel.

As an example, let's find the variance of a sample made up of 5 elements (B2:B6). To do this, you can use one of the formulas below:

=VAR(B2:B6)

=VAR.S(B2:B6)

=VARA(B2:B6)

As the screenshot shows, all the formulas return the same result (rounded to 2 decimal places):

	A	B	C	D	E	F
1	Etudiant	Note			Variance	
2	Nana	90		VAR	122,70	=VAR(B2:B11)
3	Kamga	65		VAR.S	122,70	=VAR.S(B2:B11)
4	Onana	78		VARA	122,70	=VARA(B2:B11)
5	Atangana	93				
6	Faleu	80				
7						

To check the result, let's calculate the variance manually:

1. Find the average using the AVERAGE function: **=AVERAGE(B2:B6)**

The average goes to any empty cell, say B7.

2. Subtract the average of each number in the sample: **=B2-B7**

The differences go to column C, starting with C2.

3. Square each difference and place the results in column D of , starting with D2: **=C2^2**

4. Add the differences to the square and divide the result by the number elements in the sample minus 1:

=SUM(D2:D6)/(5-1)

As you can see, the result of our manual variance calculation is exactly the same as the number returned by Excel's built-in functions:

G6 =SOMME(D2:D6)/4

	A	B	C	D	E	F	G	H
1	Etudiant	Note	Diff	Diff^2			Variance	
2	Nana	90	8,8	77,44		VAR	122,70	=VAR(B2:B11)
3	Kamga	65	-16,2	262,44		VAR.S	122,70	=VAR.S(B2:B11)
4	Onana	78	-3,2	10,24		VARA	122,70	=VARA(B2:B11)
5	Atangana	93	11,8	139,24				
6	Faleu	80	-1,2	1,44		Calcul manuel	122,70	=SOMME(D2:D11)/4
7	MOYENNE	81,2						
8								

If your dataset contains boolean and/or text values, the VARA( ) function will return a different result. The reason for this is that VAR( ) and VAR.S( ) ignore all non-number values in references, whereas VARA( ) evaluates text values as zeros, TRUE as 1 and FALSE as 0. So please choose the variance function for your calculations carefully depending on whether you want to treat or ignore text and logic.

5. How to calculate the population variance

The population is the set of members of a given group, i.e. all the observations in the field of study. The variance of the population describes the distribution of data points in the population as a whole. The variance of the population can be found using this formula:

$$Population\ variance = \frac{\sum(x - \bar{x})^2}{n}$$

Or:

- xis the population average.
- n is the size of the population, i.e. the total number of values in the population.

5. Variance formula in Excel - notes on use

To carry out the analysis of variance correctly in Excel, please follow these simple rules:

- Provide arguments in the form of values, tables or cell references ;

- In Excel 2007 and later versions, you can provide up to 255 arguments corresponding to a sample or population; in Excel 2003 and earlier versions - up to 30 arguments;
- To evaluate only the **numbers** in the references, ignoring empty cells, text and logical values, use the VAR( ) or VAR.S( ) function to calculate the variance of the sample and VAR.P( ) or VAR.P.N( ) to find the variance of the population;
- To evaluate **logical** and **textual** values in references, use the VARA( ) or VARPA( ) function;
- Supply at least **two numerical values** to a sample variance formula and at least **one numerical value** to a population variance formula in Excel, otherwise a #DIV/0! error will occur;
- Arguments containing text that cannot be interpreted as numbers cause #VALUE! errors.

Variance is undoubtedly a useful concept in science, but it gives very little practical information. For example, we found the ages of the tiger population in a local zoo and calculated the variance, which is equal to 16. The question is: how can we actually use this number?

You can use the variance to calculate the standard deviation, which is a much better measure of the amount of variation in a set of data.

The standard deviation is calculated as the square root of the variance. Done, we take the square root of 16 and obtain the standard deviation of 4.

In combination with the mean, the standard deviation can tell you how old most of the tigers are. For example, if the mean is 8 and the standard deviation is 4, most of the tigers in the zoo are between 4 years old (8 - 4) and 12 years old (8 + 4).

CHAPTER IV

INTRODUCTION TO PUBLISHER SOFTWARE

IV.1.PRESENTATION

Microsoft Office Publisher is desktop publishing software from Microsoft.

It allows you to produce communication documents of semi-professional quality.

It offers a wide range of functions:

- document creation and formatting: multiple wizards, page layout format, templates ;
- multimedia integrations with images, videos, sounds and animations.

IV.2.LAUNCHING

To launch MS Publisher, simply double-click the Publisher icon on your desktop, if you have one. Otherwise, click on the "Start" button. Point to "Programs" or "All Programs". Double-click on "Microsoft Publisher" (it may be in the "Microsoft Office" folder). Publisher opens on the "Getting Started" screen.

IV.3.PREDEFINED MODELS

The programme offers a number of predefined templates that you can modify, or allows you to create a new document from scratch.

Modelling tools

The template establishes the basis for the type of document you want to create. Editor includes many predefined templates that you can choose from whenever you create a new document. These templates often offer different variations of the same design and layout, allowing holders room for text and images. You can also change the complete colours of the template to give the same layout a completely different feel based on colour.

Text tools

Text tools are another important part of creating a Publisher file. Publisher uses floating text boxes to add text to your documents. These boxes can be resized and moved anywhere on your document. You can also choose the font style, size and colour of the text in each text box.

Image tools

Publisher lets you import clipart or other digital images into your document. Images imported as floating objects that you can move around your document and resize to fit the layout.

Editor also lets you crop a photo you've imported if you need to edit the image to focus on just a small piece instead of the whole image. The shape tool lets you place basic shapes such as circles, squares, triangles and rectangles on your document. You can change the colour and placement of these shapes and use them in the the design of your document.

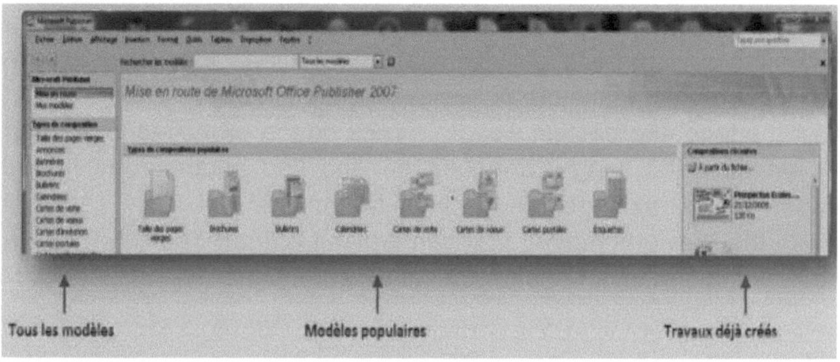

IV.4.CREATING A BUSINESS CARD

Business cards **allow professionals to pass on essential information about their company when making contact**. It is therefore essential to design them correctly and to include the most important information.

So don't hesitate to click on the second "business card" model that Publisher offers, under the "OFFERS" tab.

Classic business card with the basic "Propose" option

Stage 1

When you click on this model, the model appears on its own, in the form of a label, in the middle of the screen, along with the "create" icon. Once you have clicked on the icon, the template takes up the entire screen.

Which makes it very easy to customise.

Stage 2

To insert your personal information, simply place your cursor over any of the "text blocks" in your template and click on the small "i" square that appears.

A dialog box appears.

By clicking on the "edit professional information" line, then on the "edit" tab, you can make the desired insertions and save them.

As for the logo, the easiest way is to click on the proposed logo, then click on the "edit image" line and go and find another one in the "images" file, for example, and click on the "insert" tab.

As with the previous model, you can leave it at that. You now have a matrix for making your business cards which is perfectly acceptable.

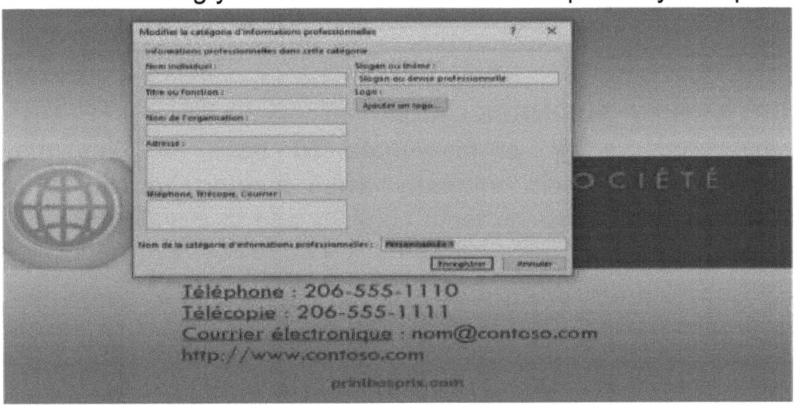

Personalising your business card

Step 3: change the font and colours

However, if, as with the previous model, you want to change the font or colour of your business card, you can also do this by clicking on the "page creation" tab in the menu bar.

Changing the details and colours of your business card

It's up to you to choose between the proposed colour schemes, for example, Apex or median, and the fonts, for example, Apex or Debit.

The rendering is particularly well done.

Step 4: Make a double-sided business card with Publisher :

Similarly, if you want to add a reverse side to your business card, open the file corresponding to the front side you've just created.

Then right-click on the page of your business card in the "Pages" column on the left of your screen. A dialogue box will appear starting with "Insert a page ...".

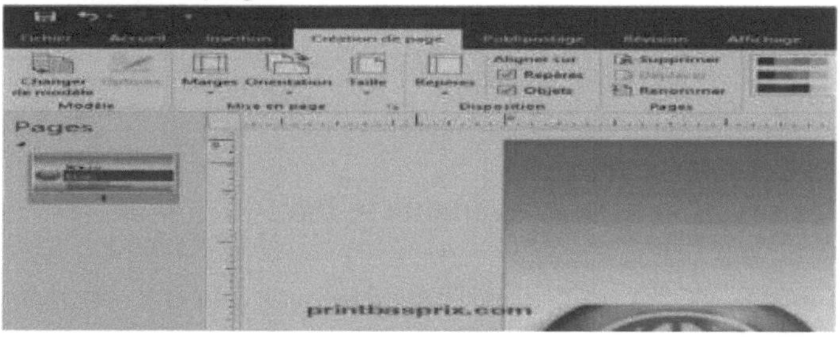

This involves inserting a page to add a reverse side to your business card on Publisher.

Clicking on "insert page" opens a new dialogue box. To insert your company's slogan or a location map on the back of your business card, for example, simply tick :

. The "after the current page" line

. And the line "create a text zone on each page".

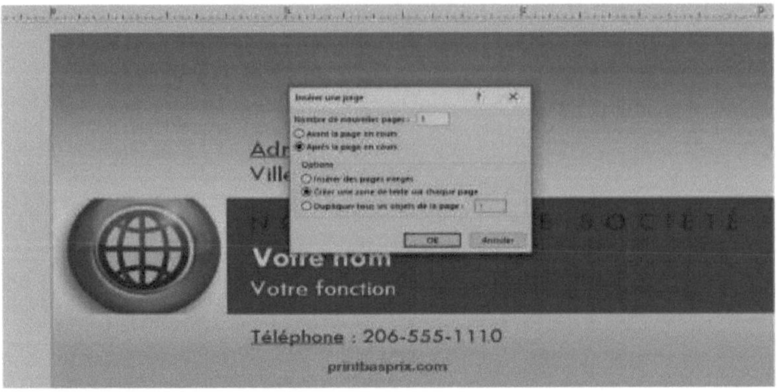

- Inserting the reverse side
- Then click OK.

It's up to you to insert the text you want in the free box that appears in full screen, then save it.

Personalise the back of your card

The other customisation modes available in the "PREDEFINI

There are two types. When you open Publisher, you need to click on the "PREDEFINI" tab. On the second line of the screen, you will see Simply click on the "business cards" icon.

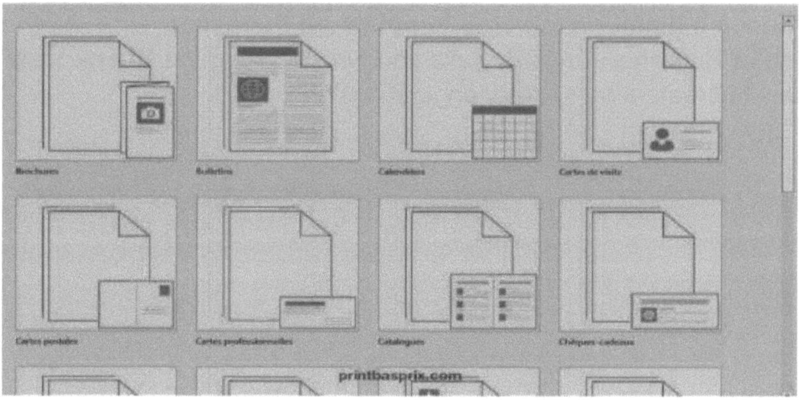

PREDEFINI" tab business card on Publisher

Choosing an integrated model

You can now choose one of the **53 built-in templates** available in Publisher by clicking on the corresponding icon.

The selected model appears in a column on the right of the screen under its reference title. By clicking on the "create" tab at the bottom of the column, you can enter your personal details.

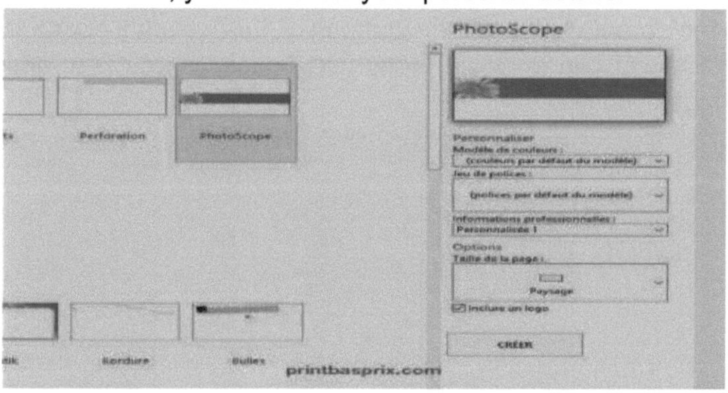

Choose from the 53 integrated double-sided business card templates

The procedure to follow is identical to that for the previous personalisation. Place the cursor over each of the "text blocks" and a small square with an "i" will appear, indicating that you can right-click.

Once you've done that, all you have to do is click on the "edit professional details" line, then on "edit", and finally, afterwards, on "save", to complete your personalisation.

As in the two previous cases, you can leave it at that, or take your customisation a step further by using the same optional commands.

A. Choose a blank recto-verso template on Publisher

If none of Publisher's models suits you, you can use the "**blank size**" formats to create a completely original design.

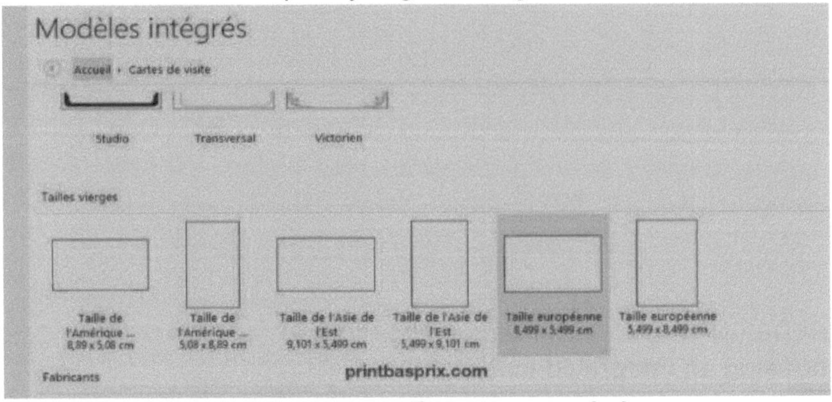

B. Choose a blank model and a European card size

visit

By clicking on the "European size" icon, a column opens on the right of the screen, under this reference heading.

Clicking on the "create" icon at the bottom of this column opens a space on which you can draw as many text boxes as you like, and insert any images you like.

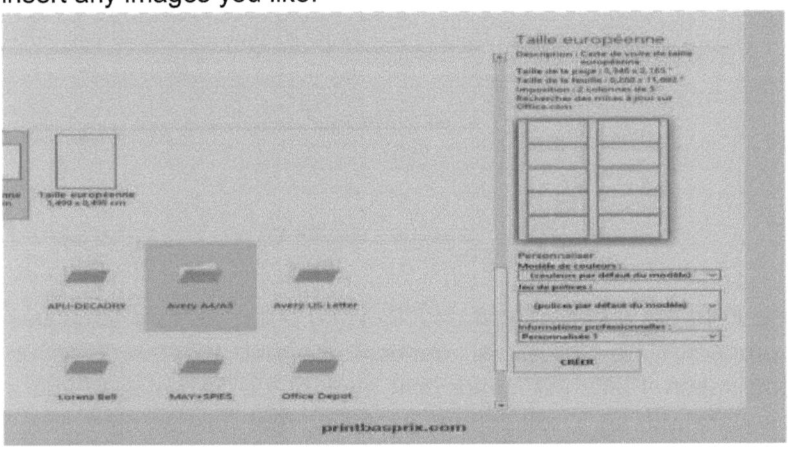

IV.5.CREATING A MAP

Choose a model

1. Start Publisher and choose a card category.

- In Publisher 2016 and Publisher 2013, click on **Greeting cards or** invitation **cards** > **integrated**.

○ In Publisher 2010, click on **Greeting cards** or **Invitation cards** in the list of templates.

2. Scroll through the predefined card publications. When you find one you like, click on it to see a larger preview.

3. Under **Customise** and **Options**, you can change a number of presentation elements before opening the composition:

○ Under **Customise**, click on the colour scheme and font set of your choice.

○ Under **Customise**, click on the business information category of your choice or create a new one.

○ Under **Options**, select the desired page size, for example **Half page with side fold** or **Quarter page with top fold**.

○ Under **Options**, select the desired layout.

Note: If you are using a template downloaded from Office Online, you cannot customise the presentation without opening the composition.

4. Click on **Create**.

Personalise your card

- Making global modifications to a model
- Using images
- Using text

Making global modifications to a model

Would you like to make changes to the entire composition? For example, you might like to try different colour schemes or fonts. You can make these changes at any time, but it's best to do so before inserting the text and images.

Do one of the following:

- To try another colour scheme, under the **Page creation** tab, click on the colour scheme you want. Click on the colour schemes to see how your greetings card will look if you choose this scheme.

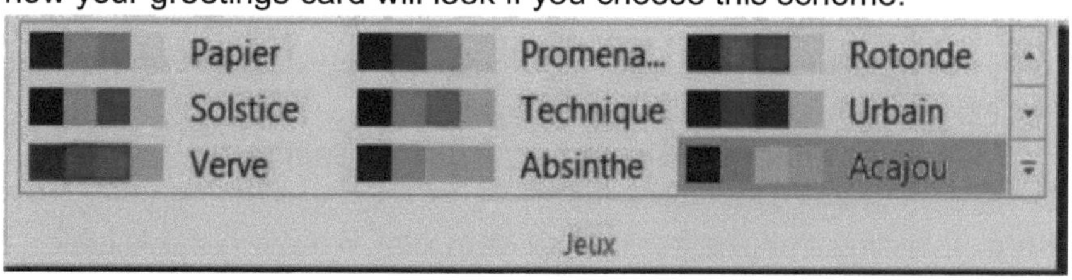

- To try another set of fonts, in the **Page Creation** tab, click **Fonts**, then choose the set you want.

. To change the page size, in the Page **Creation** tab, click **Size**, then select a new page size.

USE IMAGES

Replace image placeholders with your own images

1. Right-click on the reserve space image, then click on **Change image> Change image**.
2. In the Insert image dialogue box, search for images on your own computer or on your local network, or search for images on Office.com or from Bin.

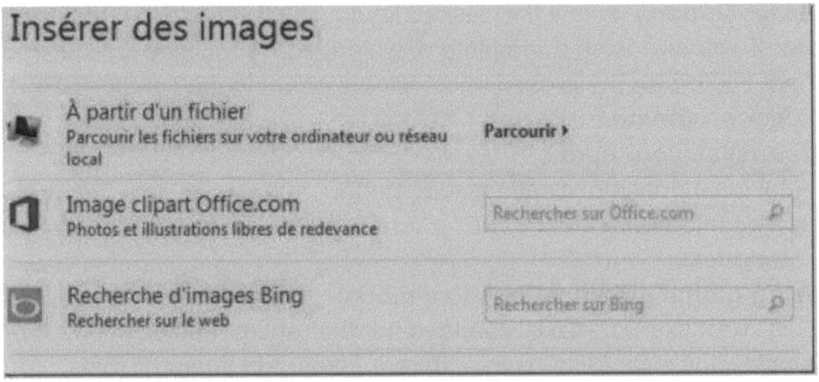

Note: Inserting images from Office.com and Bing is not available in Publisher 2010. Images found online must be downloaded to your computer before you can insert them.

3. Repeat this procedure, as required, for the other images in your composition.

Add a new image

1. In the **Insert** tab, click an image option in the **Illustrations group** (for example, **Images** or **Online Images**).
2. Search for images on your computer or search for images on Office.com or Bing, then click **Insert**.

Note: Inserting images from Office.com and Bing is not available in Publisher 2010. Images found online must be downloaded to your computer before you can insert them.

Using text

To replace the text in the reserved space with your own message, simply select the text in the reserved space, then type your own message.

Add a new text

1. On the **Insert** tab, click **Draw a text box**.
2. On your map, point to the location where you want one of the corners of the text to appear, then click and drag the cursor diagonally until you obtain an area of satisfactory size . Click in the area to type and format your text.

Replace the text in the reserve space with a formula

1. In the **Page Creation** tab, click **Options**.

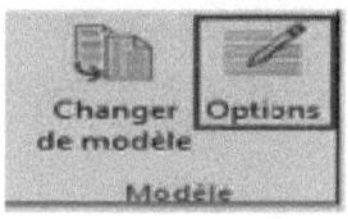

2. Under **Category**, click on the message category you want. Under **Suggested text**, click on the message you want, preview the two parts of the message on the right, then click **OK**.

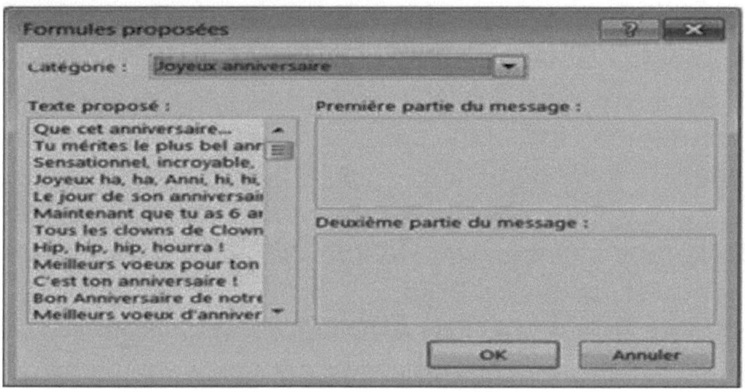

PRINT AND COMPLETE THE CARD

In Publisher, cards are configured to be printed on specific sizes of paper. For example, if you select a design which is sized for letter-size paper, you need to make two folds in the paper after printing the card.

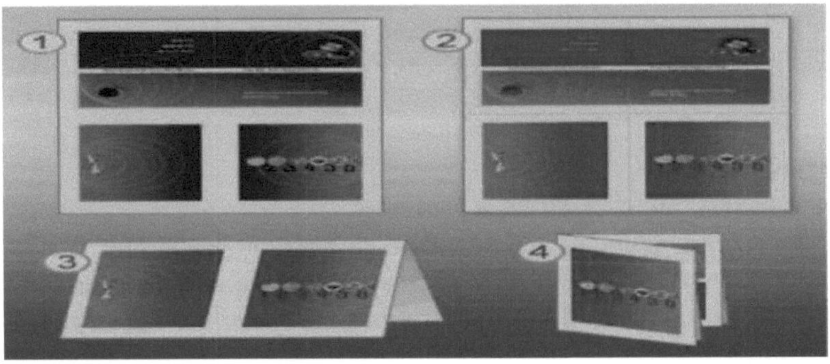

3. When you preview the card before printing it, it looks like step 1.
4. When you print the card on a colour printer, before it is folded, it looks like step 2.
5. In step 3, fold the card in half from top to bottom.
6. In step 4, you fold the card from one side to the other.

PRINT THE MAP

1. When the map looks as you want it to, save the file.
2. Click on **File>** **Print**, then, under **Settings**, check that the appropriate format is selected, such as **Side Fold, Quarter Sheet**, **Side Fold, Half Sheet** or **Booklet,** Side **Fold**.

Note: These options are only available when the page size of the composition is smaller than that of the paper on which the composition is set to be printed.

3. The preview pane shows how your composition will look on the printed page. Make any changes you want to the print options, such as the number of copies, then click **Print**.

IV.6.PROFESSIONAL INFORMATION AND LOGO

1. Click on the position in your composition where you want the logo.
2. Click **on Insert** > **professional** information **> additional professional** information.

3. Under **Logos**, click on the logo design of your choice, select the graphic and text options of your choice (for example, two lines of text with the logo), then click **Insert.**
4. To replace the text in the reserve space in the logo, select the text

in the text box, then type in the text of your choice.

5. To replace the reserve space image in the logo, click on the image frame in the logo, right-click on the image, click on Modify image, then select the image of your choice.

Note: If you want to save the building block library logo and add it to your business information set, you need to save it as a building block and then add it to a business information set.

You can open a template you have already used, modify it and save it as a new template.

1. **Click on File> New.**
2. Click on **PERSONAL**, then double-click on the name of a model.

Note: If your template is not listed, you may not have saved it in the default template location folder. The default template location is C:UtilitiesUserNameDocumentsCustomised Office *Templates*. If you have saved a template to a location other than the default template location, you must go to the location where you saved it and open the template from there or move it to the default template location on your computer.

3. Make the desired changes to the model.
4. Click on **File> Save As**, then go to drive C on your computer.
5. In the **File type** field, click **Publisher template**, then type a new name and an optional category for the template.
6. Click on **Save**.

IV.7.COMPOSITIONAL ELEMENTS

Creating a composition

All compositions start from a template, even if it's a blank one. The difficulty lies in choosing a template that is as close as possible to what you are looking for in your final composition. Publisher comes with default templates.

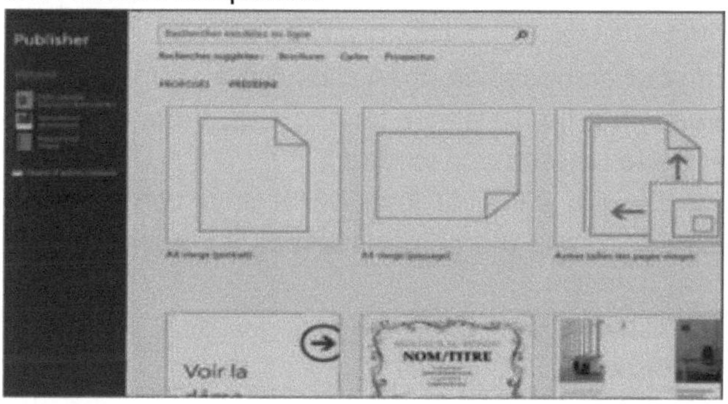

1. Click on **File>** **New**, then proceed as follows:

o Choose one of the **suggested** models and click **Create**.

o To use one of the templates installed in Publisher, choose **Default**, scroll down the list to the category you want, click on it, choose the template you want, then click **Create**.

o To find a template on Office.com, use the **Search for templates online** box to find what you want. Enter "newsletter", for example, scroll down the list to the template of your choice, then click **Create**.

Record your composition

Proceed as follows to record your composition for the first time

1. Click on **File>** **Save as**.
2. In **Save as**, choose where you want to save your composition.

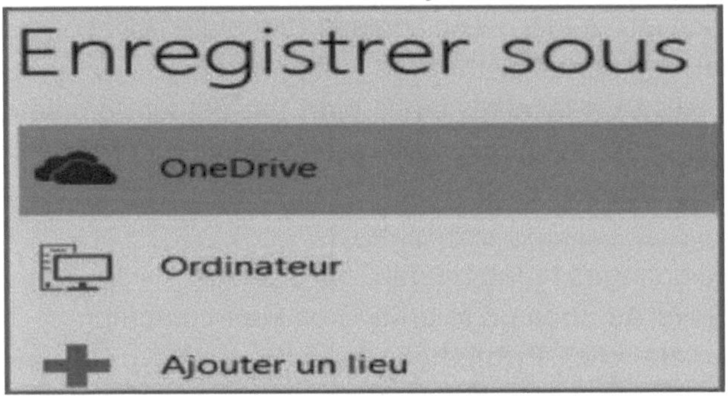

o **OneDrive** is a free Microsoft service providing password-protected online file storage.

o **Other web locations** includes websites you have used recently and a **Browse** button allowing you to save your composition on any website you access.

o **Computer** includes all the folders on your computer.

o **Add a location** lets you add an online location to save your composition.

3. Enter the name of your composition, then click **Save**.

Once you have saved your composition for the first time, you can simply click on **File>** **Save** whenever necessary.

If you want to change the file name or location of your composition, click on **File>** **Save as** and save the composition as if it were the first time.

ADDING IMAGES TO YOUR COMPOSITION

1. Click on **Home>** **Images**.
2. Use the options in the **Insert images** dialogue box to find the

image you want to use.

ADDING TEXT TO YOUR COMPOSITION

To add text to your composition, start by inserting a text box. Most templates include text boxes that you can fill in, but you can also add your own text boxes.

First step: adding a text zone

1. Click on **Home>** **Draw a text area** and drag the cross-hair cursor to draw an area where you want it.

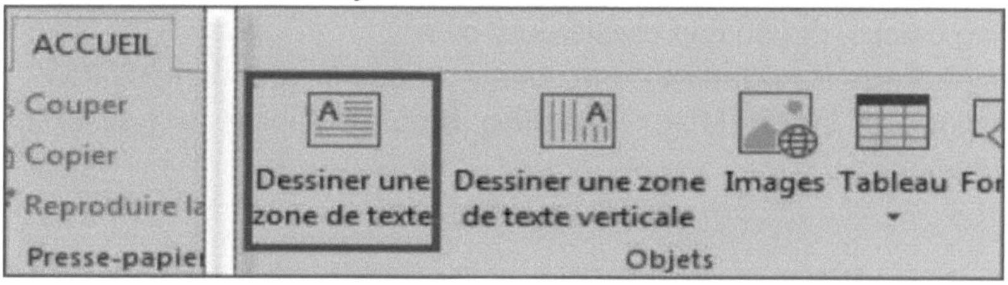

2. Type text in the text box.

If the text you are typing is too long for the text box, you can enlarge it or link it to another text box.

Second step: linking your text boxes

You can link text zones so that text flows from one zone to another.

1. When a text box contains too much text, a small area with ellipses appears at the bottom right of the text box.

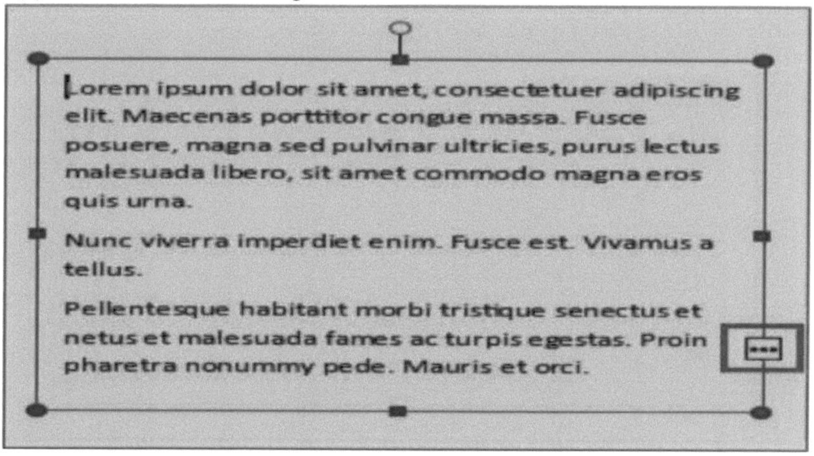

2. Create a new text zone.
3. Click on the overflow indicator to turn your cursor into a cup.
4. Move the new text box, then click.

The overflow text appears in the new text zone.

Now, when you add text, the words automatically move from one text zone to another. If you run out of space in this second text zone, you can create a link to another text zone so that the text passes through all three zones.

ADD BUILDING BLOCKS TO YOUR COMPOSITION

Building blocks are reusable parts of content, such as titles, calendars, borders and advertisements. Publisher offers default building blocks, or you can create your own.

1. In the **Page Navigation** pane, select a page in your composition.
2. Under the **Insert** tab> **Building blocks**, choose a gallery of building blocks.

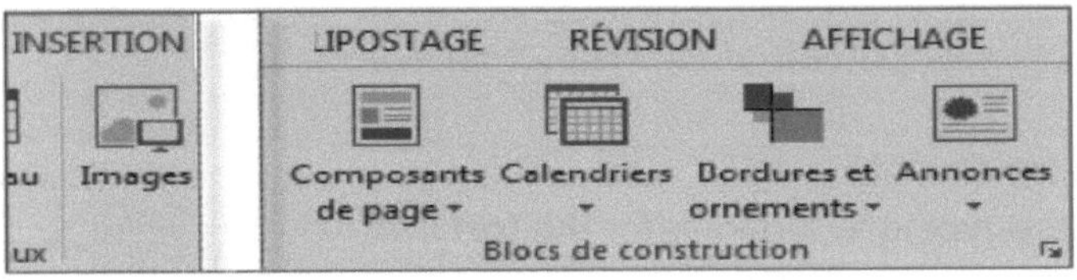

3. Scroll to find a building block, or click on **Other <gallery name>** to open **Building Block Library**.
4. Click on a building block.

6. Print your composition

1. Click on **File> Print**.

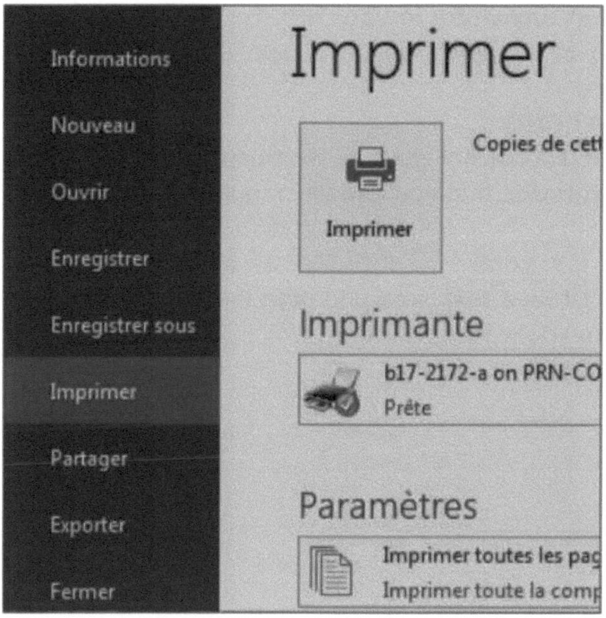

2. Under **Print**, enter the number of copies to print in the **Copies** field **for this print job**.
3. Check that the correct printer is selected.

Note: The default printer properties are automatically entered for you.

4. Under **Settings**, proceed as follows:

- Check that the correct range of pages or sections has been selected.
- Select a page setup format for printing.
- Set the paper size.
- Define single-sided or double-sided printing.
- If your printer can print in colour, choose either colour or greyscale printing.

Click on the **Print** button when you are ready to print.

IV .8.WORKING IN TEXT ZONES

V V.8.1.DEFINITION

(IT) **Widget for entering or simply displaying text** (usually fairly short) .[†]

VI .8.2.ROLE OF THE TEXT ZONE

A text box is an object you can add to your document that **allows you**

[†] https://www.lalanguefrancaise.com, consulted on 26/10/2023 at 06h24'.

to place and type text anywhere in your file. Text boxes are useful for drawing attention to a specific piece of text or for moving text around your document.

VII 8.3.TEXT FORMATTING

To add text to your composition, start by inserting a text box. Most templates include text boxes that you can fill in, but you can also add your own text boxes.

First step: adding a text zone

1. Click on **Home> Draw a text area** and drag the cross-hair cursor to draw an area where you want it.

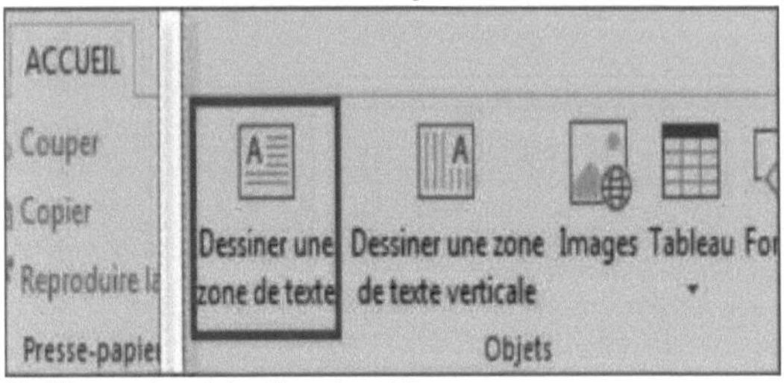

2. Type text in the text box.

If the text you are typing is too long for the text box, you can enlarge it or link it to another text box.

Second step: linking your text boxes

You can link text zones so that text flows from one zone to another.

1. When a text box contains too much text, a small area with ellipses appears at the bottom right of the text box.

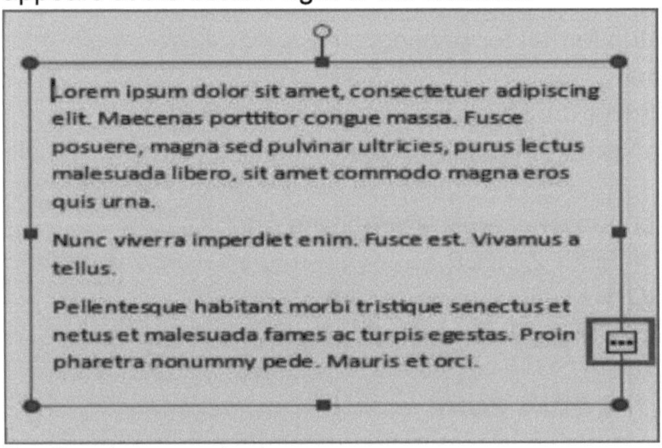

2. Create a new text zone.
3. Click on the overflow indicator to turn your cursor into a cup [x]

4. Move the new text box, then click.

The overflow text appears in the new text zone.

Now, when you add text, the words automatically move from one text zone to another. If you run out of space in this second text zone, you can create a link to another text zone so that the text passes through all three zones.

IV.8.4.PAGE LAYOUT

You can **print your Publisher documents** easily, but first you need to do the **layout**, and that's what you'll learn in this tutorial.

You can easily *change the layout of a Publisher document and print it out*, simply by following the steps below: **Step 1**: Open Publisher and then open a document by clicking on "file" after "new" (in our example we are using a blank document□

If you already have a document, click on "File" then "Open" and choose your . □

Step 2: Click on "File" then "Layout" to display the layout modification window. In the "layout" tab, you can change the type of composition, size and orientation.

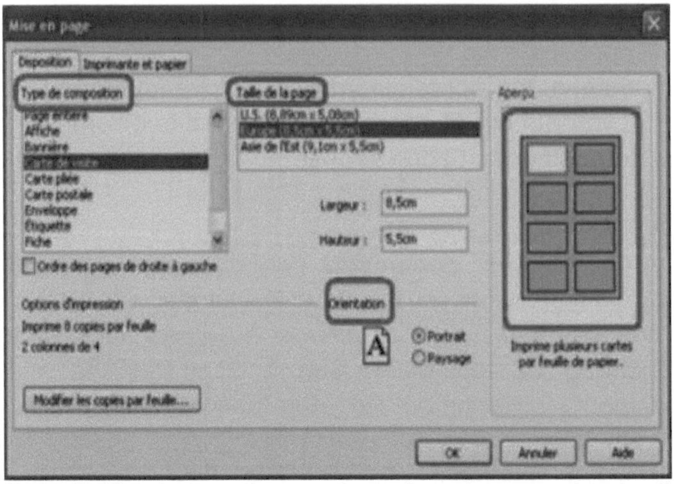

Step 3: To change the number of copies per sheet, click on "change copies per sheet".

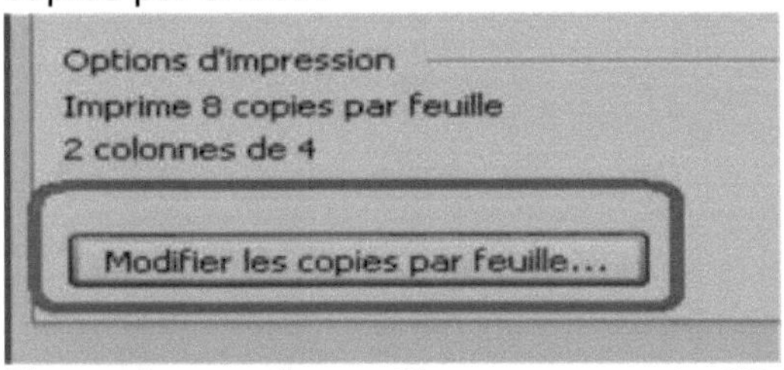

Then change the settings you want. Click on "ok" when you have finished.

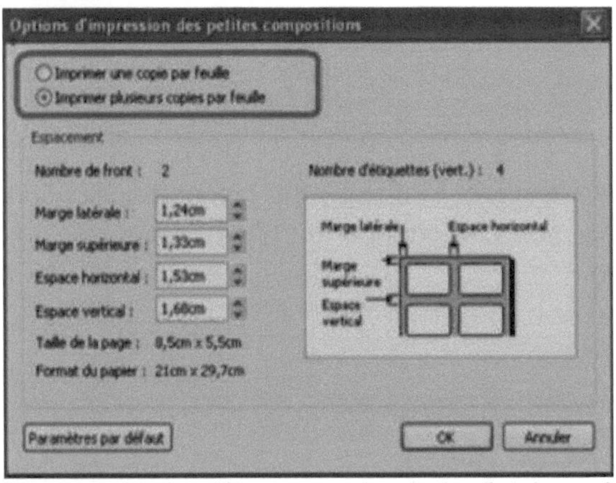

Step 4: In the "Paper and printing" tab, select the size of the print sheet.

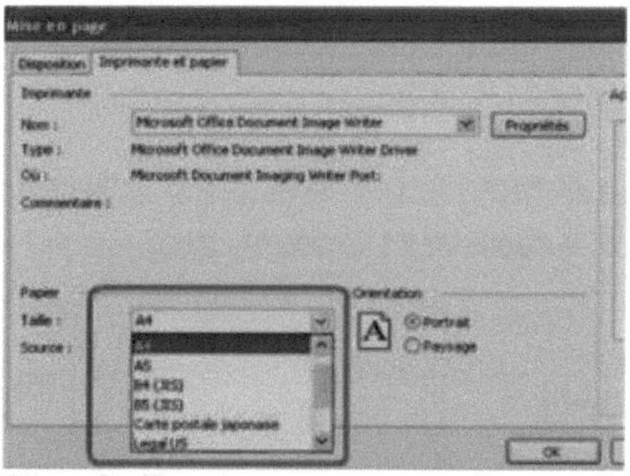

Step 5: Preview your page for printing by clicking on "File" then "**Print preview"**.

IV .8.5 EXERCISES

CHAPTER V

COMPOSITION OF A POSTER

V .1.DEFINITION OF A POSTER

A poster is a printed sheet intended to bring something to the attention of the public and posted on walls or in reserved places .‡

VI 2.INSERTING WORDART

1. Go to **Insert> WordArt**
2. Choose the WordArt style you want.
3. Enter your text.

Note: To convert an existing text into a WordArt object, select the text, *then* select **Insert> WordArt**.

Change the colour

1. Select the WordArt text you want to modify.
2. In **Shape format** or **Drawing tools**, select **Text fill** or **Text outline**, then choose the desired colour.

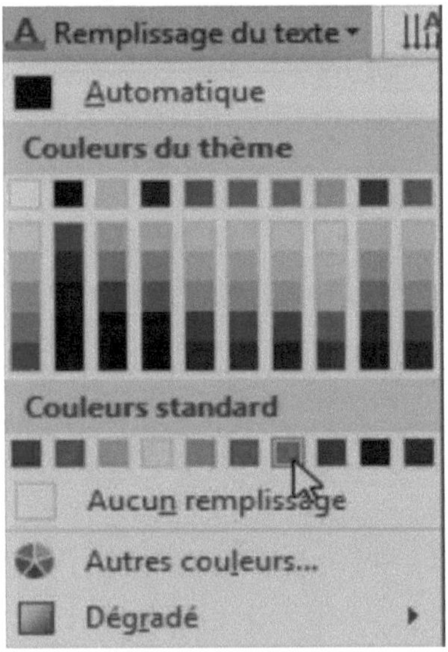

‡ https://www.google.com, consulted on 26/10/2023 at 06h40'.

3. Click outside your text box to see the effect.

Choose a text effect

1. Select the WordArt text you want to modify.
2. Go to **Shape format** or Design **tools** - Format > **Text effects** > Transform.

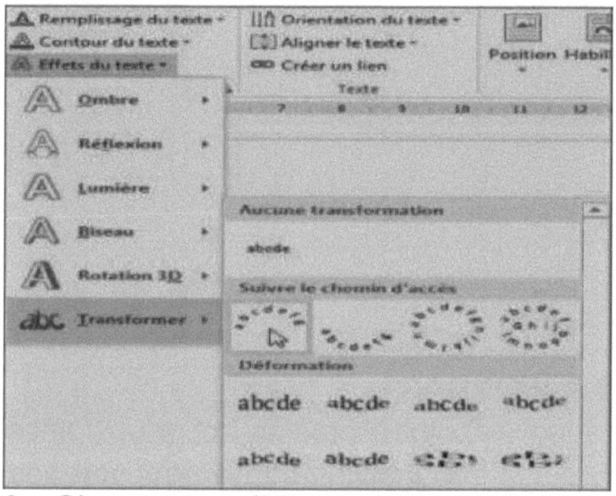

3. Choose the effect you want.
4. Click outside your text box to see the effect.

Rotate

1. Select the WordArt object, then drag the circular rotation handle to the top of the area.

2. To flip a WordArt object or rotate it 90 degrees, go to **Format** or **Drawing tools Format> Rotate**, then select an option.

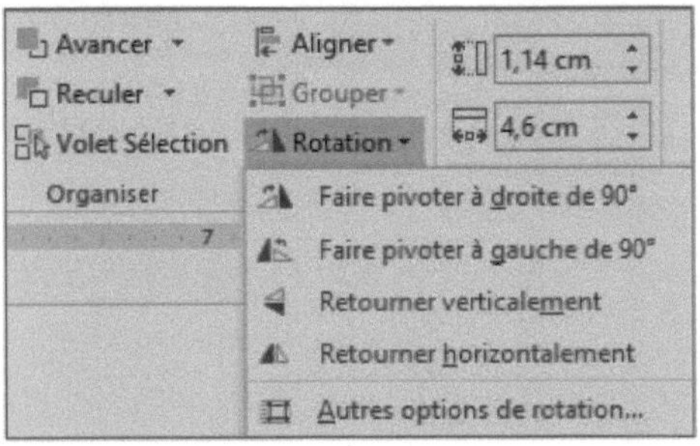

V.3.MOVING AND ALIGNING A WORDART

When you add images, shapes or other objects to your Office documents, they automatically stack into individual layers as you add them. You can move individual shapes or other objects or groups of objects within a stack. For example, you can move objects up or down in a stack one layer at a time, or you can move them up or down a stack in a single move. You can overlap objects as you draw to create different effects.

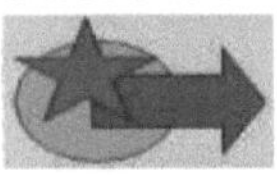

Moving an image, shape, text box or WordArt element

1. Click on the border of the WordArt object, text box or shape to be moved.

To move several text areas or shapes, hold down the Ctrl key while clicking on the borders.

2. When the cursor changes to a four-pointed arrow, drag it to the new

location.

To move the object in small increments, hold down the Ctrl key while pressing an arrow key. To move the object horizontally or vertically only, hold down the Shift key while dragging the object.

Note: The incremental distance, or spacing, is an increment of 1 pixel. What this screen pixel represents in relation to the document area depends on the zoom factor. When you zoom in on your document at 400%, one screen pixel is a relatively small zoom distance on the document. When you zoom out on your document to 25%, one screen pixel is a relatively large zoom distance on the document.

Depending on the state of movement of the WordArt art, shape or text area, it may be easier to cut and paste it. Right-click on the object, then click **Cut** (or press Ctrl+X). Press Ctrl+V to paste it. You can also cut and paste them into another document or between programs, for example, from PowerPoint to Excel calculation.

Move a text zone, WordArt or shape forwards or backwards in a stack

1. Click on the WordArt object, shape or text box you want to move up or down in the stack.
2. On the **Drawing tools** tab, click **Move forward** or **Move back**.

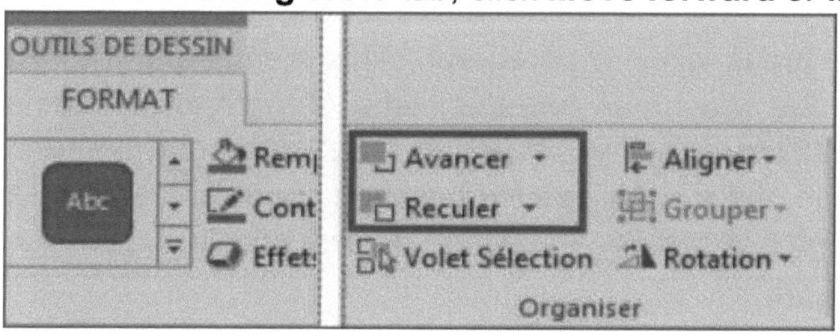

You can move the object up one level (**Move Up**) or to the top of the stack (**Move to Foreground**). **Move back** offers similar options: move down one level (**Move back**) or to the bottom of the stack (**Move to background**).

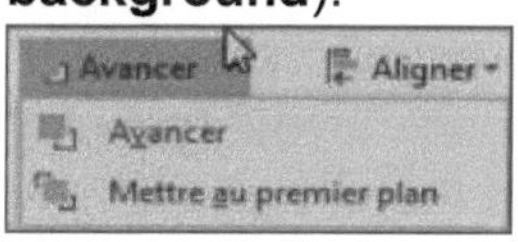

NB: In Office 2016 and Office 2013, if you have a large number of WordArt objects, shapes, text boxes or other objects, it may be easier to use the up and down arrows in the Selection pane to move objects. The **Selection Pane** is not available in Project or Office 2010.

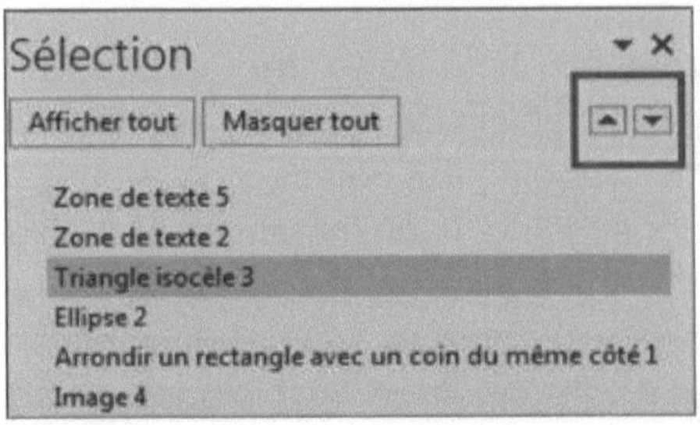

V.4.NON-PRINTABLE CHARACTERS

A. Non-printable characters

A non-printable character is a character that may appear on screen but is not printed. This type of character gives information about the formatting of the text. To make non-printable characters appear on screen, click on the icon in the shape of the paragraph mark.

There are many non-printable characters. Here are the best known

Paragraph mark: ¶

It indicates the end of a paragraph and a line break. To insert a paragraph mark, simply press [Enter].

Line feed : ↵

It indicates a line break within a paragraph. This means that the text before and after the line break has the same paragraph formatting (alignment, indentation, spacing). As a line break does not mark the end of a paragraph, there is no spacing between lines separated by a line break (although it is possible to change the line spacing).

The tabulation mark →

It indicates where the tab key has been pressed (the two horizontal arrows on the left of the keyboard). Combined with a tab stop, the tab stop allows text to be placed anywhere on the line. If no tab stop has been placed, Word uses invisible tab stops every 1.25 cm.

V.5.DUPLICATION OF SHAPES

Use the Copy Layout tool to copy the fill and layout of one shape to another in just a few clicks. Note that the Reproduce layout tool only copies the visual layout; it does not copy any data that the shape may contain.

Copy the layout using the Copy layout tool

1. Right-click on the shape with the layout you want to copy, then in the mini-toolbar, click **Copy layout**.

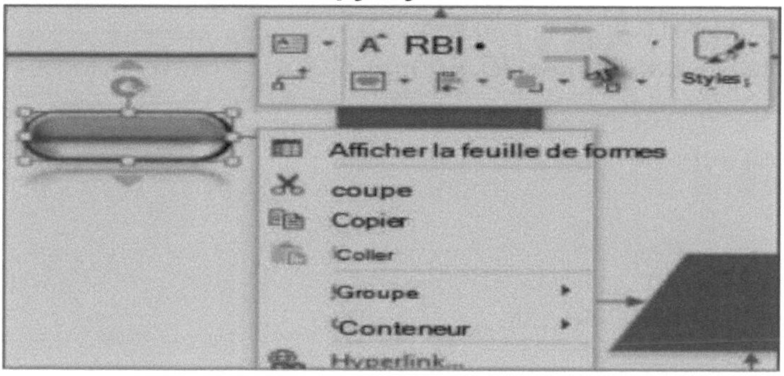

Your pointer changes to an A This means that the next object you click on gets the formatting of the first form.

2. Click on another shape. The copied layout is applied to the second form.

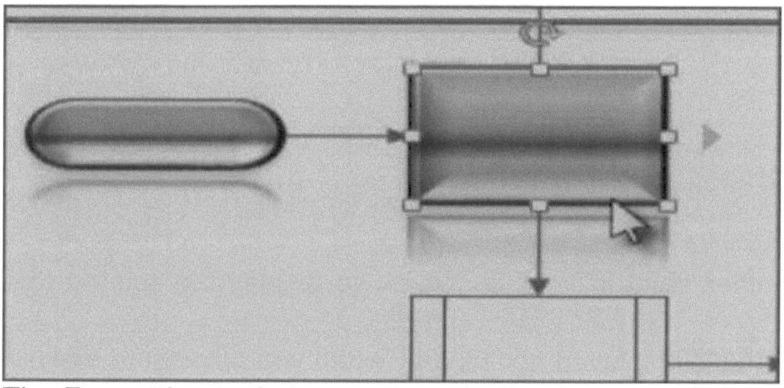

The Formatting tool stops automatically when you click on the second shape and the formatting has been applied.

Tip: If you change your mind before clicking on the second shape, press Esc to deactivate the Shaping tool.

Copy the layout of several shapes

To modify several shapes, click on the shape you want to copy, then hold down the mouse while clicking on the shapes to be modified. Then right-click, and click **Shape**. All the shapes you click on will take on the formatting of the first shape you clicked on.

If the different shapes are grouped together, click on the shape to be copied, click on Copy layout, **then** click on the group. The layout is applied to each shape in the group at the same time.

V.6.ROTATING A TEXT ZONE

To rotate text in Word, first place the text in a text box and then rotate the text box.

1. Select a text zoneTo do this, you can :

◦ Select the text area, then select **Format** shape or Drawing tools **> Rotate.**

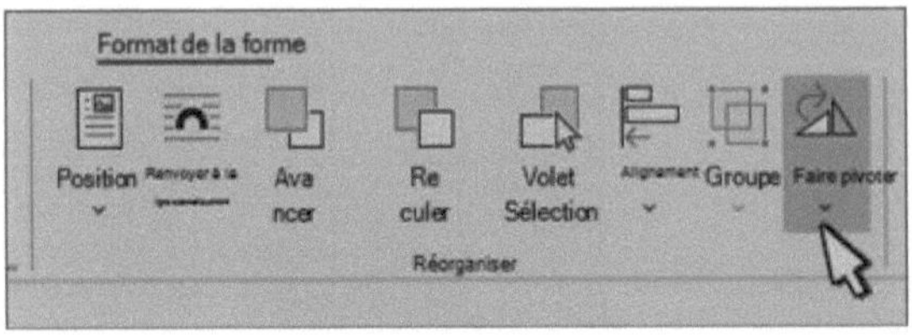

Use one of the rotation commands in the list.

◦ Manually rotate the text area by selecting the text area rotation handle and dragging in the direction of your choice. To keep the rotation at 15 degree angles, hold down Lat verso while dragging the rotation handle.

2. Select another point in your document to display the rotated text area.

Note: A text box is displayed horizontally when you select it to make it easier to edit the text.

Mirroring text in a text box

The inversion of a line or paragraph of text in a text zone.

1. Select the text zone.
2. Select **Shape format** or **Design tools - Format.**
3. Select Text **effects** B> **3D rotation** options> **3D rotation options.**
4. Under **3D Rotation,** set **the X rotation to 180°.**

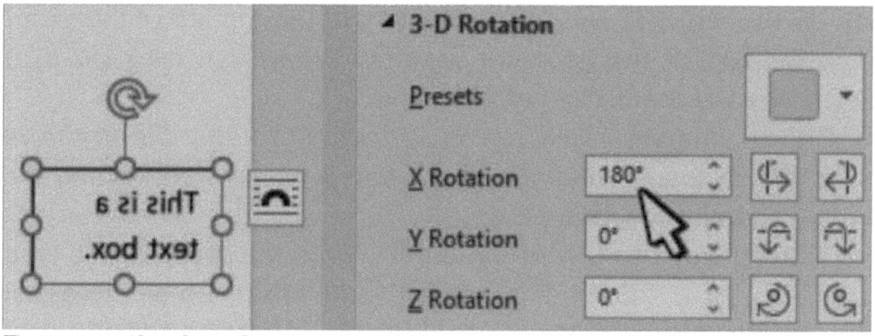

Remove the border

1. Select the text zone.
2. Select **Shape format** or Design **tools** - Format > Shape **outline**, then **select No outline.**

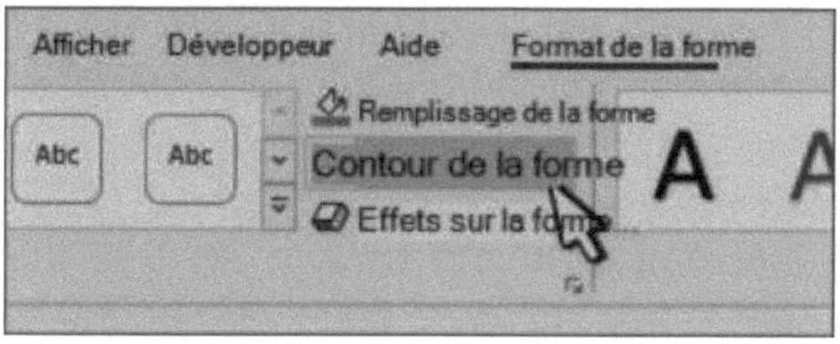

The border around the text box disappears when you click or tap outside the text box.

Modify the border

1. Select the border of the text zone.
2. Go to Shape **format** or Drawing tools **- Format** > Shape outline to change the outline colour, to change the stroke weight or to change the stroke to dashes.

Display Developer Help Form format

Filling the shape Contouring the shape Q) Effects on the fqmfc...

3. Select **Effects on the** shape to add a shadow or light to the border.

V.7.INSERTING CLIPART

Learn how to insert clipart into a Word document on macOS and Windows. Although the clipart functionality of older versions of Office has been replaced by Bing images, you could still search for and insert clipart in a Word document.

1. **Open a Word document.** Double-click on the file to which you want to add the clipart.
   - You can also create a new document by double-clicking on the Microsoft Word icon, then selecting ***Blank document***.

2. **Click on the INSERT tab.** You will find it at the top left of the Word ribbon at the top of the program window. When you click on it, a toolbar will open at the bottom of the menu.

Select Online images. This option is located in the ***Illustrations*** section of the toolbar. When you click on it, a window containing the Bing image search bar will appear.

Enter a search word followed by clipart. Type the name of the type of image you want followed by clipart, and press Enter. This will launch a search in Bing for images that match your keyword.

- To find elephant clipart, for example, you would type elephant clipart and press Enter.
- Please note, however, that you must have an Internet connection before you can search for images on Bing.

Choose an image. Click on the clipart you would like to use in your Word document. You will then see a tick in the top left-hand corner of the image, showing that you have selected it.

- You could select several images at once.

Click on Insert. You'll find this button at the bottom right of the window. When you click on it, the image will immediately be added to your Word document.

CHAPTER VI

CREATING FORMS WITH WORD

A form is a **document containing fixed and variable fields for users to complete**.

Below, we'll show you how to create a Word form that can be filled in by other people:

Step 1: Go to the "Developer" section

. Go to the "File" tab, then click on "Options".

. Now select "Customise the ribbon". And go to the list under "Main tabs", tick the "Developer" box, then click "OK".

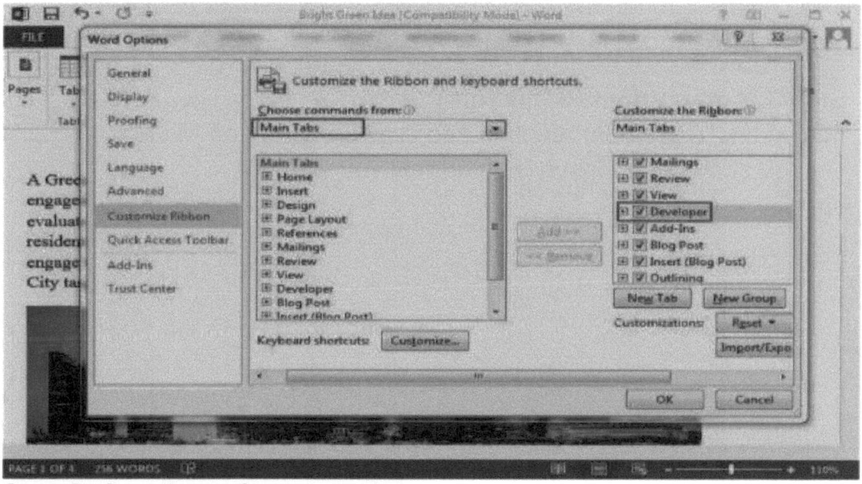

Step 2: Creating a form template

To avoid wasting time, we recommend that you start with a sample form. You can also start with a blank template.

A model form: your starting point

. Go to the "File" section and click on "New".

. You will see a "Search for models online" box. Here, indicate the type of form you wish to create and click "ENTER".

- Select the desired form and click on "Create".

To start with a blank model :

. Go to the "File" tab and click on "New".

- Click on "Blank document".

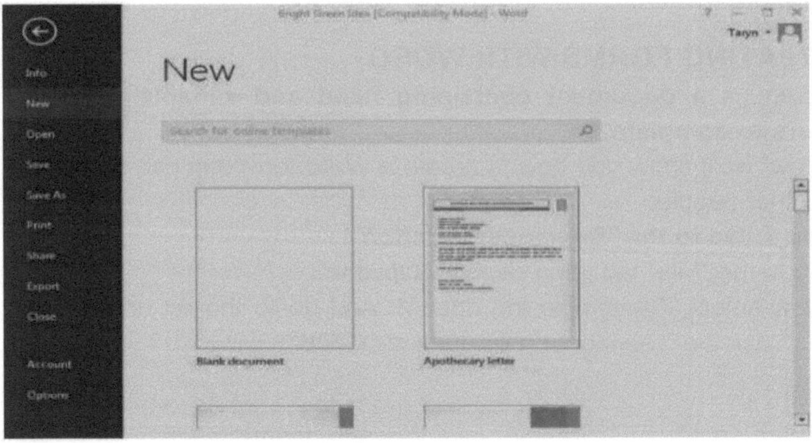

Step 3: Add content to this form

. Go to the "Developer" section and click on "Creation Mode".

- You should then insert the controls you want

apply.

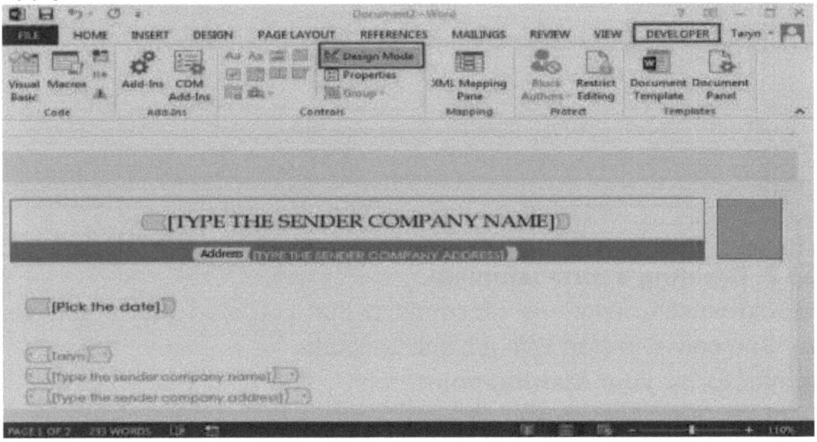

You need to insert a text control in a section where users can enter text.

Users can format text in italics or bold using a rich text content control. They can also type several paragraphs. If you want to limit what users can add, you need to enter (or better still, insert) a plain text content control.

- Click on the part in which you wish to insert this control.
- Go to the "Developer" section, then select "Plain text content control" or "Rich text content control".

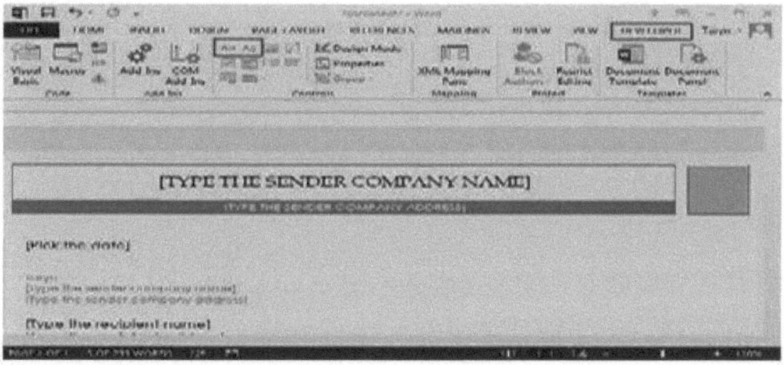

Step 4: Defining content control properties

You can define/modify certain properties for all content controls.

- Select the content control (image, date selector, etc.) you wish to modify.

. Go to the "Developer" section, click on "Properties" to select the desired properties.

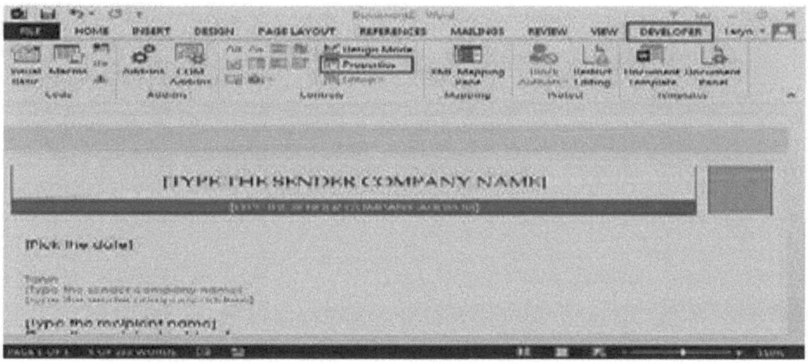

Step 5: Include an instruction text in your form

Proceed as follows to customise the default instruction text for users of the form: . Go to the "Developer" section and select "Creation Mode".

• Click on the content control in which you wish to modify the instruction text for the reserved space.

• Apply the desired change to the substitution text and apply the formatting in the style you prefer.

. Once again, go to the "Developer" section and untick "Creation Mode" to disable the design function and save the instruction text you have added.

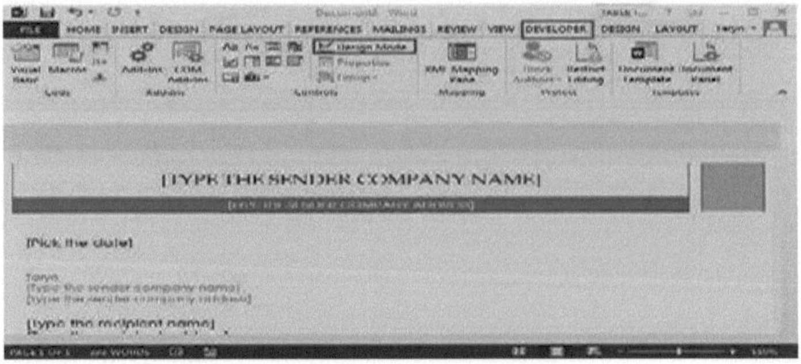

Step 6: Include protection in your form

This step (using the "Restrict editing" command) allows you to limit the possibility of others formatting/editing your form:

- Open your form to go to "Home", click on "Select" and then press CTRL + A on your keyboard.

. Go to the "Developer" tab and select "Restrict publishing".

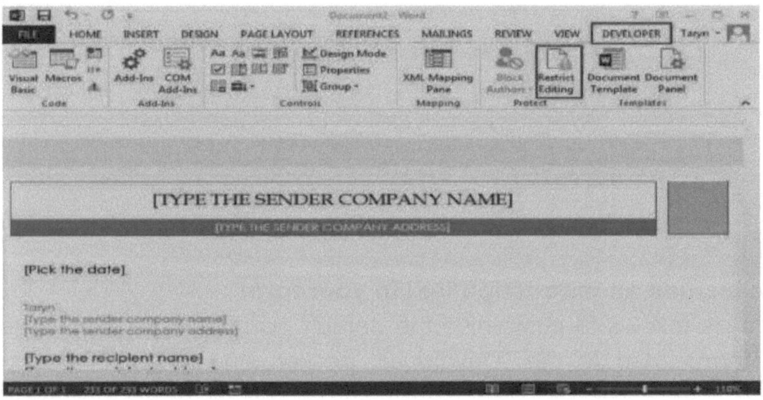

CHAPTER VII

ANTIVIRUS SOFTWARE

VII.1.DEFINITION OF CONCEPTS

Software: All the programmes and procedures required to run a computer system.

Antivirus: Software utility that detects and destroys computer viruses that attack a computer's memory.

VII.2.INSTALLATION

It is essential to follow a strict procedure when installing antivirus software on your computer.

Most anti-virus software is available to download from their manufacturers' websites. If you have not yet installed such software, or if none has been installed by default by the computer manufacturer, it is essential to install one yourself. However, it is dangerous to download antivirus software from a computer that is not protected by such a programme.

The safest and most highly recommended solution is therefore to download it from a computer that is already protected by an antivirus and then save it on a USB stick. You can then install it on the computer you want to protect without running the risk of catching a virus. To do this, make sure that the unprotected computer is isolated from the Internet, as it could be the target of a hacker attack during the installation phase.

To do this, simply deactivate the network connection in the computer's control panel or, if this is the case, simply unplug the socket that connects the computer to the network. Once the antivirus has been installed from the programme on the USB stick, the computer can be reconnected to the Internet. The computer already benefits from a good level of protection, even if all the latest virus definitions have not yet been installed.

You should be aware that the publishers of this software are improving their software almost daily to keep up with the inventiveness of Internet pirates in infecting and gaining access to computers connected to the Internet. It is therefore advisable to immediately carry out the updates proposed by the software publishers. Depending on their settings, these updates are carried out (which is usually the case) fully automatically, without users even noticing.

Below is a (non-exhaustive) list of some of the most popular antivirus software on the market:

Software name	**Publisher**	**Free/Paid**	**Where can I download it?**
Avast	Avast	Free and paying	www.avast.com
AVG	AVG	Free/Paid	www.avg.com
Bit Defender	Bit Defender	Paying	www.bitdefender.fr
Kaspersky	Kaspersky	Paying	www.kaspersky.com
McAfee	McAfee	Paying	www.mcafee.com
Microsoft Security Essentials	Microsoft	Free	www.microsoft.fr
Norton Antivirus	Symantec	Paying	www.symantec.com
Windows Defender	Microsoft	Free	www.microsoft.com

Some anti-virus software are free, while others have to be paid for.

Even publishers of free software offer versions that are more powerful or offer more extensive functions, but which have to be paid for. Very often, you have to look hard on the publishers' websites to find out where and how to download the free version of their software, because they make a point of encouraging you to download a paid version. Some software is free to use for a certain period of time (e.g. 30 days), so that you can test it before buying it. Others are totally free, at least for the time being, but this could change depending on their success or the commercial strategy of their publishers.

Some anti-virus software also incorporates a so-called "firewall" module that provides protection to prevent hackers from penetrating your computer by locking the doors that let them in. This is, of course, absolutely essential protection. If the antivirus software you choose does not also offer this protection, you will also need to install firewall software.

On the other hand, it is totally inadvisable to install several anti-virus or firewall programs on the same computer, as this can lead to blockages and will not improve the level of protection of your computer.

Among the various anti-virus programs, Microsoft's (called Microsoft Security Essentials in Windows 7 versions and Windows Defender from Windows 8 and 10) offers a very good level of protection, even though it is free, without being too resource-hungry, i.e. it does not slow down your computer too much when it is running and updates are being made. So you can carry on working almost unnoticed while it's running. These two anti-virus programs, which are updated with regular Windows updates, are automatically deactivated as soon as another anti-virus program is installed, and are reactivated if a third-party anti-virus program is uninstalled.

Some older software packages have grown in size over the years and are becoming increasingly complex and resource-hungry. They therefore slow down work or, at the very least, slow down the start-up and operation of computers. The risk is that some impatient users may be tempted to deactivate their antivirus software to make their work easier.

INSTALLING ANTIVIRUS SOFTWARE ON WINDOWS

Whatever antivirus you choose, installation and configuration on a Windows device is fairly similar. Here's how to do it:

1. **Create an account**

It is not always necessary to create an account straight away, but it will be practical in the long term. With some publishers it is not necessary to register immediately, but it will be required within 30 days of purchase. Creating an account will give you direct access to updates, and allow you to manage your licences and other features, such as remote anti-theft functionality for your mobile device, in one place.

2. **Download the antivirus**

Click to download the antivirus. It will usually tell you how much space you need, so you may need to delete some files to free up space.

3. **Authorise changes**

It is also crucial to check that you have administrator privileges, as you will need to authorise the installation of the software. This step requires you to enter your password via an administrator account. It sounds complicated, but chances are you're already the administrator and Windows will simply authorise the installation when you run it. Just give it a try.

4. **Follow the on-screen installation process**

The software will then guide you through a short installation process, which usually involves accepting the terms and conditions of use and defining where the antivirus will be registered. The installer will walk you through these steps.

5. **Restart your computer**

The version you downloaded may not be the most recent. Simply restart your computer, which will display all the updates you need to install. Once that's done, run a full scan of your computer

VII .3.USE

Malicious people or organisations sometimes try to steal personal data using spyware or viruses. Most of the time, these attacks are aimed at recovering bank details, secret documents, confidential data, etc.

To protect against these attacks and viruses that could destroy your system, **antivirus** software has been developed. However, you can also find antivirus software on Android, for your smartphone or tablet.

As well as anti-virus software to combat attacks and clean up your system, it is also advisable **to activate a firewall**.

However, it should be noted that using antivirus software is not always enough to protect you from viruses or malware. Its **settings and use** are just as important to ensure that your antivirus software detects suspicious files and places them in quarantine.

Using the antivirus with interesting options

Before choosing any antivirus, it is important to **identify how you use your computer**: do you leave it on 24 hours a day? Do you download often? Do you regularly visit high-risk sites? Do you tend to install programmes you don't know where they come from? Based on your answers, you can start looking for an antivirus.

With antivirus software, malicious software and viruses stored on your hard drive can be detected. But more comprehensive solutions also offer an effective **firewall** to protect your computer from attack. Some antivirus solutions can also scan your RAM, your incoming and outgoing e-mails and your boot sector. These different options mean you can better ward off dangers and risks.

Another important point: your antivirus software must be able to **quarantine** files that could be affected and damaged by a virus. So it's best to be careful!

Identify potential infections

When you install your antivirus software, don't forget to set up **a scan of your files** on removable media and the hard disk. This will help identify any malicious software.

To activate this scan policy, go to the configuration area of your antivirus software. Once set, the scan will scan all the files accessible on your hard disk and USB devices.

Please note, however, that running this scan **will decrease the performance of your computer**. If you are running an application that uses a lot of CPU capacity, for example, the scan will render your PC unusable. So run a scan in such a way that it does not interfere with the use of your computer.

Finally, check that files are **quarantined and not** automatically **deleted.** Your antivirus software may consider a file to be a virus even though it is healthy.

ANTI-VIRUS UPDATE POLICIES

When using your antivirus software, don't forget to check that it is **up to date** and can protect your system over time. In general, antivirus software is based on a database of identified viruses. This database is updated regularly, as new viruses are developed every week by hackers.

With some antivirus software, this **update is done automatically**. With this system, you don't have to worry about forgetting: it's done automatically. If this option is available, remember to activate it. If not, set up a memo so that you can do it yourself manually.

You now have all the information you need to use your antivirus software properly. By following these few tips, your computer will be protected from attacks and viruses and attempts to recover your personal data will be minimised. With antivirus software, you can surf the Internet with peace of mind!

CHAPTER VIII

CONDITIONAL FORMATTING WITH EXCEL

You can use conditional formatting to highlight cells that contain values corresponding to a condition. Or, you can format an entire range of cells and vary the formatting according to the values in each of the cells.

Temperature information with conditional formatting displaying 10% of the highest values and 10% of the lowest values

	A	B	C	D	E	F	G	H	I	J	K	L	M
1		Janv	Févr	Mars	Avr	Mai	Juin	Juil	Août	Sep	Oct	Nov	Déc
2	Moy. ht	4	3	7	8	11	13	19	22	21	15	7	5
3	Moy. bs	1	1	4	5	7	9	11	13	12	7	5	3

Temperature information with conditional shading in 3 colours:

	A	B	C	D	E	F	G	H	I	J	K	L	M
1		Jan	Feb	Mar	Apr	May	Jun	Jul	Aug	Sep	Oct	Nov	Dec
2	Avg Hi	40	38	44	46	51	56	67	72	70	59	45	41
3	Avg Lo	34	33	39	41	45	48	51	55	54	45	41	38

VIII.1.APPLY CONDITIONAL FORMATTING

1. Select the range of cells, the table or the whole sheet where you want to apply conditional formatting.
2. On the **Home** tab, click **Conditional formatting**.

VIII.2.CONDITIONS ON FORMULAS

Function SI.CONDITIONS

The SI.CONDITIONS function checks whether one or more conditions are met and returns a value corresponding to the first true condition. Using this function is like using several nested SI statements, but it is much easier to read when several conditions follow each other.

Simple syntax

The SI.CONDITIONS function generally uses the following syntax: *=SI.CONDITIONS([logic_test1; true_value1; logic_test2; true_value2; logic_test3;true_value3)*

The SI.CONDITIONS function allows you to test up to 127 different conditions. However, we do not recommend nesting too many conditions with SI or SI.CONDITIONS statements. It is not advisable to use too many conditions, however, as they must be entered in the correct order. They can also be difficult to create, test and update.

Example 1

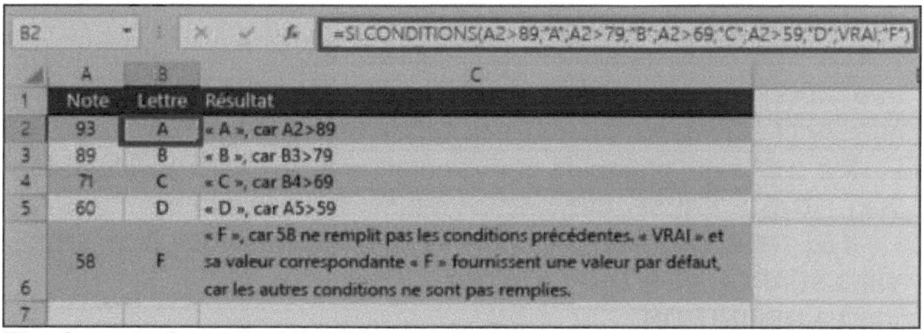

B2 | =SI.CONDITIONS(A2>89;"A";A2>79;"B";A2>69;"C";A2>59;"D";VRAI;"F")

	A	B	C
1	Note	Lettre	Résultat
2	93	A	« A », car A2>89
3	89	B	« B », car B3>79
4	71	C	« C », car B4>69
5	60	D	« D », car A5>59
6	58	F	« F », car 58 ne remplit pas les conditions précédentes. « VRAI » et sa valeur correspondante « F » fournissent une valeur par défaut, car les autres conditions ne sont pas remplies.
7			

The formula for cells A2:A6 is as follows:

=SI.CONDITIONS(A2>89;"A";A2>79;"B";A2>69;"C";A2>59;"D";VRAI;"
F")

The formula has the following meaning: *SI.CONDITIONS(A2 is greater than 89, return the value "A"; IF A2 is greater than 79, return the value "B"; etc. and for all other values less than 59, return the value "F").*

Example 2

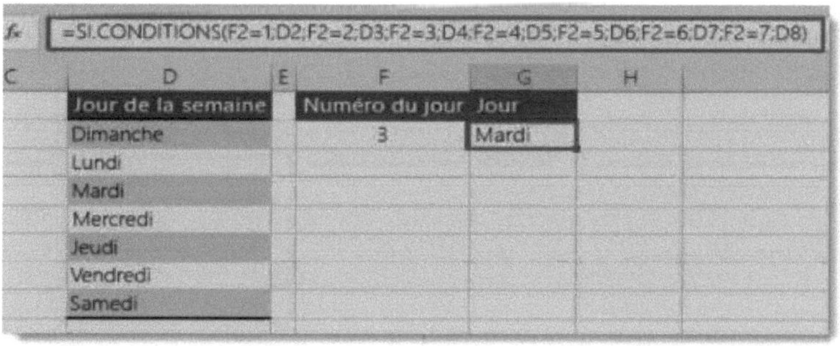

=SI.CONDITIONS(F2=1;D2;F2=2;D3;F2=3;D4;F2=4;D5;F2=5;D6;F2=6;D7;F2=7;D8)

D	E	F	G
Jour de la semaine		Numéro du jour	Jour
Dimanche		3	Mardi
Lundi			
Mardi			
Mercredi			
Jeudi			
Vendredi			
Samedi			

The formula in cell G7 is :

=SI.CONDITIONS(F2=1;D2;F2=2;D3;F2=3;D4;F2=4;D5;F2=5;D6;F2=
6;
D7;F2=7;D8)

The formula has the following meaning: *IF(the value in cell F2 is equal to 1, return the value in cell D2; IF the value in cell F2 is equal to 2, return the value in cell D3; etc., ending with the value in cell D8 if no other condition is met).*

Remarks

- To specify a default result, enter TRUE for your final logical_test argument. If no other conditions are met, the corresponding value will be returned. This result is shown on lines 6 and 7 (with note 58) of the first example.

. If a *test_logic* argument is supplied without a corresponding *true_value* argument, this function returns the error message "The number of arguments entered is insufficient for this function".

- If a *test_logic* argument is evaluated and results in a value other than TRUE or FALSE, this function returns a #VALUE! error.
- If no TRUE condition is found, this function returns the error #N/A.

VIII.3.SEARCH FOR DUPLICATES

VIII.3.1.DEFINITION

A duplicate is a typographical error, a repetition of an element of the manuscript (word, sentence, etc.). Something in duplicate, which doubles .[§]

Sometimes duplicate data is useful, but other times it just makes your data harder to understand. Use conditional formatting to search for and highlight duplicate data. This way, you can review the duplicates and decide whether you want to delete them.

1. Select the cells in which you want to check the presence of duplicates.

Note: Excel cannot highlight duplicates in the Values area of a pivot table report.

§ https://dictionnaire.lerobert.com, consulted on 27/10/2023 at 04h24'.

2. Select **Home>** **Conditional formatting>** **Highlight cells> duplicate values**.

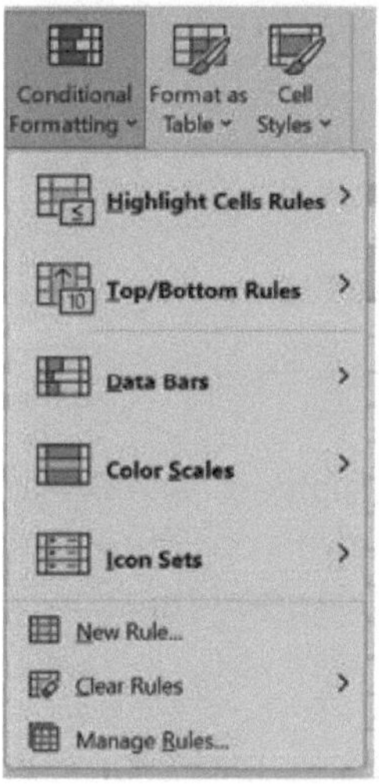

3. In the box next to **values with**, select the formatting you wish to apply to the duplicated values, then select **OK.**

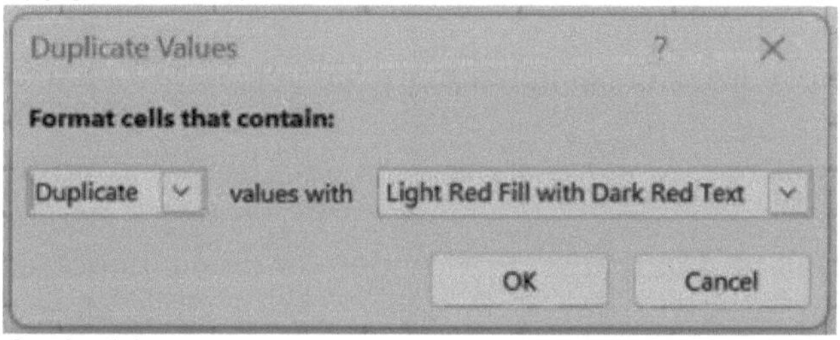

Or do this;

1. select the area in which you want to delete duplicates Excel ;
2. click on the conditional formatting icon. The option is represented by an icon with several small red and blue boxes of different sizes;
3. select the "cell highlighting rules" option ;
4. scroll down to the bottom of the open contextual tab and click on Duplicate values.

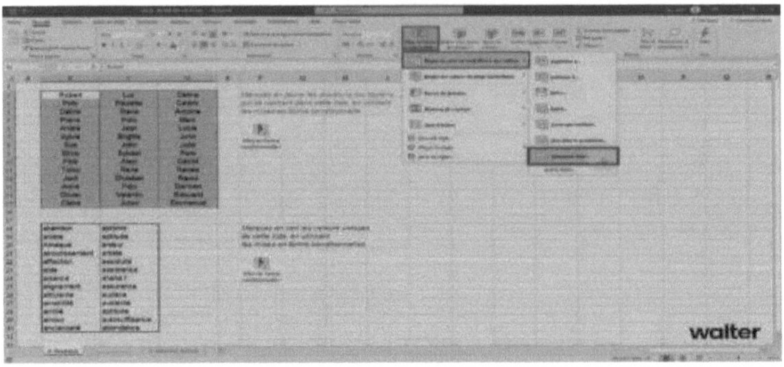

You'll see the duplicates in the selected area highlighted. Thanks to an open pop-up window, you can select the colour of your choice to indicate duplicates. This system allows you to quickly see duplicates or larger numbers of values.

DELETE DUPLICATE VALUES

When you use the **Delete Duplicates** function, duplicate data is permanently deleted. Before deleting duplicates, it's a good idea to copy the original data to another worksheet so that you don't inadvertently lose any information.

1. Select the range of cells containing the duplicate values you want to delete.

Tip: Remove any outlines or subtotals in your data before trying to remove duplicates.

2. Select **Data>** **Delete duplicates**, then under **Columns**, check or uncheck the boxes for the columns in which you wish to delete duplicates.

For example, in this spreadsheet, the January column contains price information that I want to keep.

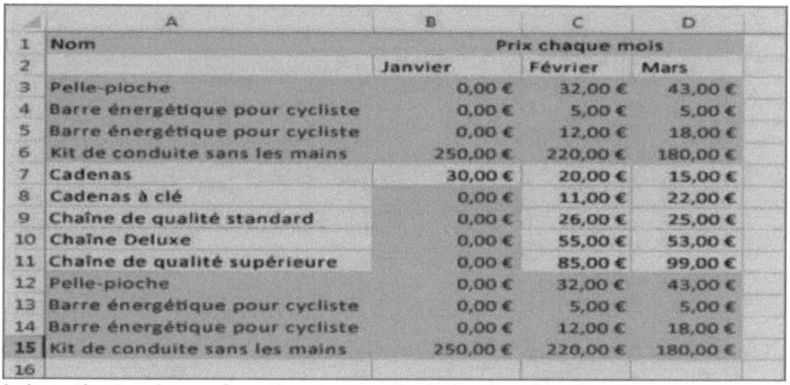

	A	B	C	D
1	Nom	Prix chaque mois		
2		Janvier	Février	Mars
3	Pelle-pioche	0,00 €	32,00 €	43,00 €
4	Barre énergétique pour cycliste	0,00 €	5,00 €	5,00 €
5	Barre énergétique pour cycliste	0,00 €	12,00 €	18,00 €
6	Kit de conduite sans les mains	250,00 €	220,00 €	180,00 €
7	Cadenas	30,00 €	20,00 €	15,00 €
8	Cadenas à clé	0,00 €	11,00 €	22,00 €
9	Chaîne de qualité standard	0,00 €	26,00 €	25,00 €
10	Chaîne Deluxe	0,00 €	55,00 €	53,00 €
11	Chaîne de qualité supérieure	0,00 €	85,00 €	99,00 €
12	Pelle-pioche	0,00 €	32,00 €	43,00 €
13	Barre énergétique pour cycliste	0,00 €	5,00 €	5,00 €
14	Barre énergétique pour cycliste	0,00 €	12,00 €	18,00 €
15	Kit de conduite sans les mains	250,00 €	220,00 €	180,00 €
16				

I deactivate done **Janvier** in the **Delete duplicates** box.

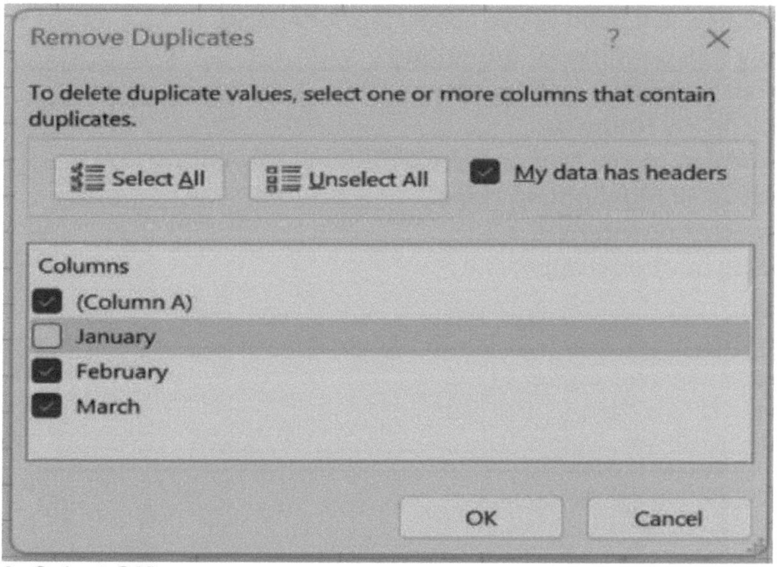

3. Select **OK**.

Note: The number of unique and duplicate values shown after deletion may include empty cells, spaces, etc.

VIII.4.CONDITIONAL FORMATTING AND SORTING

VIII.4.1.CONDITIONAL FORMATTING

In addition to what we saw earlier, **Conditional Formatting** also lets you define the layout of a cell if a condition is met in the content of that cell.

For example, in the turnover table, you want values under €100,000 to be highlighted in red.

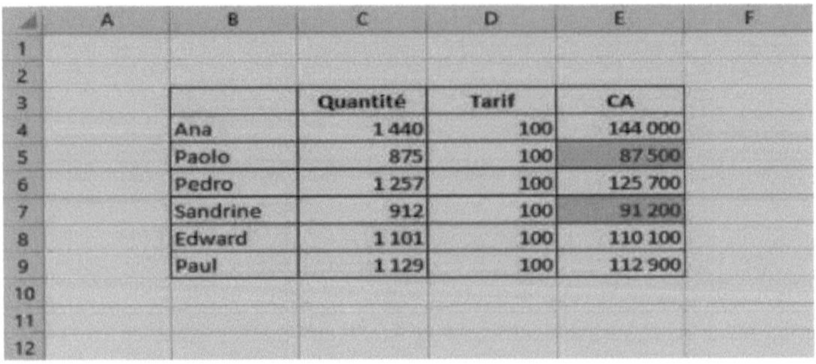

	Quantité	Tarif	CA
Ana	1 440	100	144 000
Paolo	875	100	87 500
Pedro	1 257	100	125 700
Sandrine	912	100	91 200
Edward	1 101	100	110 100
Paul	1 129	100	112 900

Turnover of less than €100,000 is shown in red

Of course, you could colour in the cells that meet the condition (below 100,000 euros), but in this case, if the figure changes and goes above 100,000 euros, the cell will retain the layout and remain in red.

To avoid this, you need to use conditional formatting.

To **apply this conditional formatting** :

- Select the cells to be formatted.
- Click on the **Home** tab.

. In the **Styles** group, click on the **Conditional formatting** icon

- Select **Cell highlighting rules**.
- Then click on **Inferieur a...**

The dialog box below appears:

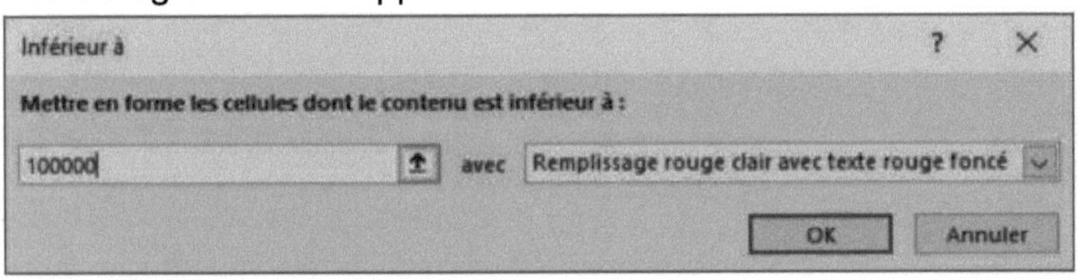

Enter 100000 in the dialog box

❖ Click OK to validate your conditional formatting.

When you click OK, the formatting you have defined is applied to the cells that meet the condition, i.e. those below 100,000 euros.

If you want to remove the automatic formatting, proceed as follows:

❖ Select the cells to be formatted.

❖ Click on the **Home** tab.

❖ In the **Styles** group, click on the **Conditional formatting** icon.

❖ Select **Delete rules**.

❖ Then click **Clear rules from selected cells**.

In the following example, you will show three coloured indicators according to turnover.

	Quantité	Tarif	CA
Ana	1 440	100	144 000
Paolo	875	100	87 500
Pedro	1 257	100	125 700
Sandrine	912	100	91 200
Edward	1 101	100	110 100
Paul	1 129	100	112 900

Conditional formatting with 3 indicators

To **apply this conditional formatting** :

- Select the cells to be formatted.
- Click on the **Home** tab.
- In the **Styles** group, click on the **Conditional formatting** icon.
- Select **Icon sets**.
- In **Shapes**, select **3 indicators (without borders)**.

Conditional formatting is very useful for highlighting elements when a condition is met. It has a wide range of uses, and there are many possibilities. I'll leave you to discover all its potential and get creative!

VIII.4.2.TRIS

VIII.4.2.1.SORTING DATA QUICKLY IN EXCEL

This is the simplest case: you want to sort your data table according to the values in a single column. Whether that column contains text, numbers, dates or times, the principle is exactly the same. For the example, we'll take a column of text.

Your table may or may not contain column headings, Excel detects if there are any and is rarely wrong. The best thing would still be to add them systematically to make your tables more comprehensible. Below, our column headers are called *City, Region* and *Turnover.*

Ville	Région	Chiffre d'affaires
Pau	Nouvelle-Aquitaine	393 801 €
Toulouse	Occitanie	222 661 €
Nice	PACA	463 202 €
Aix-en-Provence	PACA	234 149 €
Perpignan	Occitanie	360 725 €
Bayonne	Nouvelle-Aquitaine	316 896 €
Avignon	PACA	189 053 €
La Rochelle	Nouvelle-Aquitaine	318 879 €

The same sorting options can be found in different places in the Excel menus, so here we'll show you four methods, all equally quick - use the one you like. And it goes without saying that they all produce the same result!

To sort a table according to the values in a column, click on any **single cell** in that column. For example, click on a cell in the *Town* column to sort the towns alphabetically.

. **Method 1 -** Under the **Home** tab, click on **Sort and Filter > Sort from A to Z** to sort in ascending order, or on **Sort from Z to A** to sort in descending order.

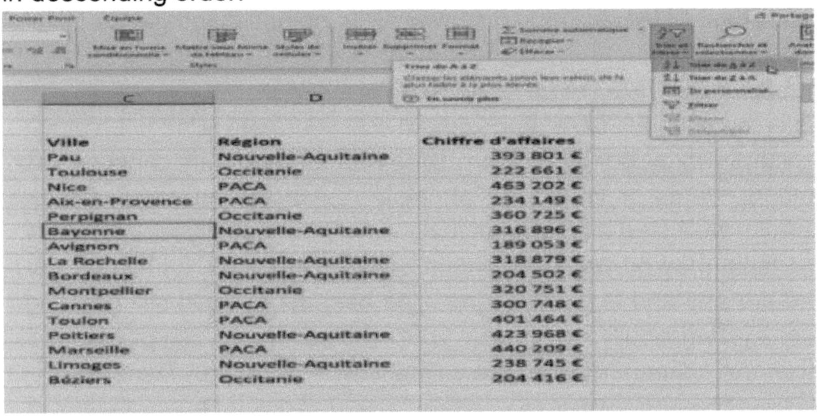

. Even if you have only selected one cell, Excel takes the whole table into account: each line is therefore sorted, here in ascending alphabetical order on the name of the town.

Ville	Région	Chiffre d'affaires
Aix-en-Provence	PACA	234 149 €
Avignon	PACA	189 053 €
Bayonne	Nouvelle-Aquitaine	316 896 €
Béziers	Occitanie	204 416 €
Bordeaux	Nouvelle-Aquitaine	204 502 €
Cannes	PACA	300 748 €
La Rochelle	Nouvelle-Aquitaine	318 879 €
Limoges	Nouvelle-Aquitaine	238 745 €
Marseille	PACA	440 209 €
Montpellier	Occitanie	320 751 €
Nice	PACA	463 202 €
Pau	Nouvelle-Aquitaine	393 801 €
Perpignan	Occitanie	360 725 €
Poitiers	Nouvelle-Aquitaine	423 968 €
Toulon	PACA	401 464 €
Toulouse	Occitanie	222 661 €

Method 2 - Right-click on any cell in the column to be sorted, and select **Sort > Sort A to Z** from the context menu. Below, the *Region* column is sorted.

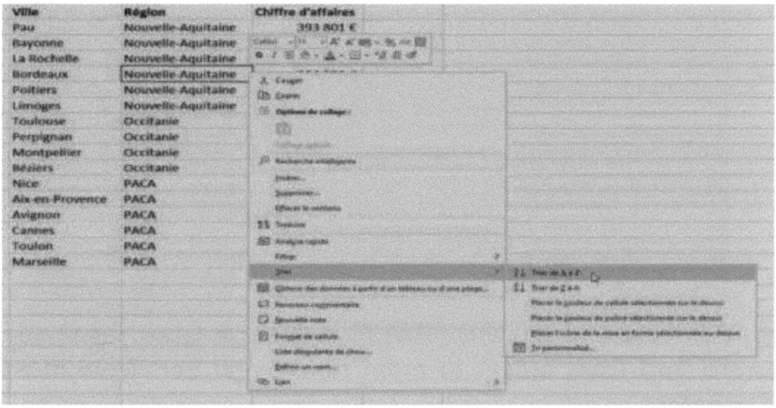

. Method 3 - Click on any cell in the column to be sorted and, under the **Data** tab, click on the **Sort from A to Z** (ascending order), **Sort from Z to A** (descending order) or **Sort** icon to display the custom sorting window.

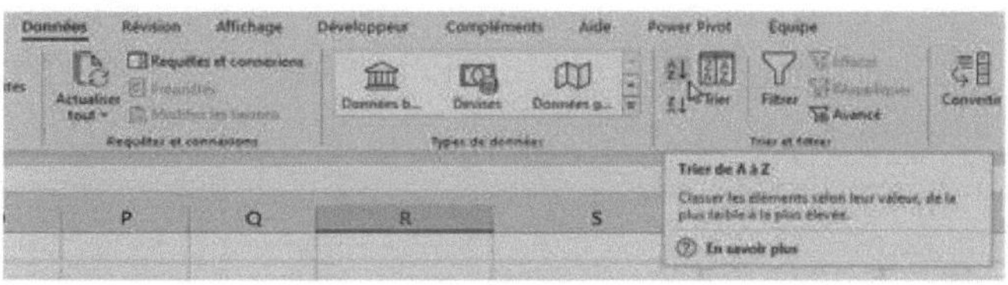

. Method 4 - If you have activated the filters in your table, for example via the **Home > Sort and filter > Filter** tab, click on a filter button in the header row and choose **Sort from A to Z** or **Sort from Z to A**.

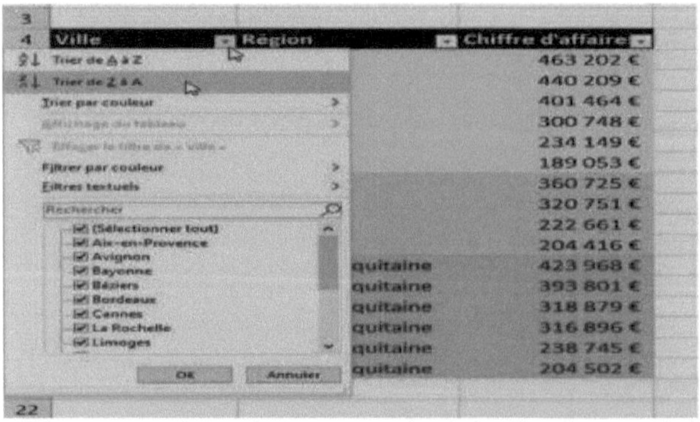

. The spreadsheet menus adapt to the type of data. If Excel detects that the column used as a sort criterion contains numbers or times, the choices are **Sort smallest to largest** or **Sort largest to smallest**.

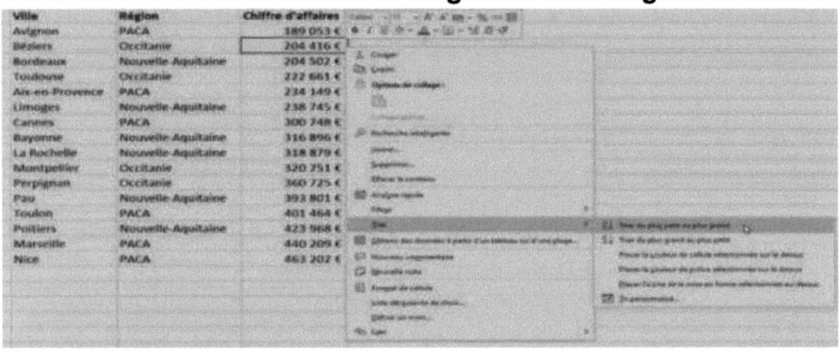

- And if the column contains numeric values of type "date", the choices are **Sort from oldest to most recent** and **Sort from most recent to oldest.**

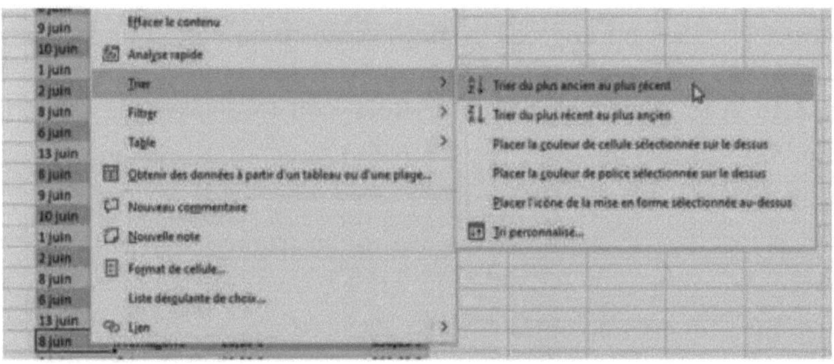

- Discard always a look at the result. The sorting did not work

correctly? Start by undoing it: press **Ctrl+Z** on a PC or **Cmd+Z** on a Mac to undo the last action(s). You can also use the **Undo** button at the top left of the Excel window, which shows you a list of the last actions that can be undone (note: this list applies to this workbook and all the files currently open in Excel!)

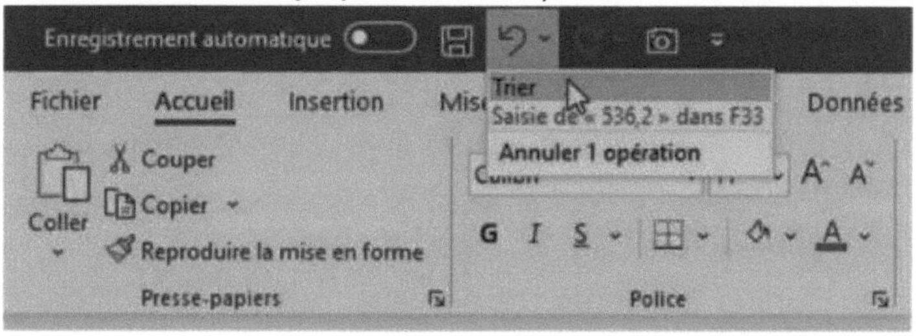

. Note: if a cell in the sort column is empty, Excel returns the whole row at the end of the table. Below, after sorting on city names, the row without a city name is dropped at the end of the table.

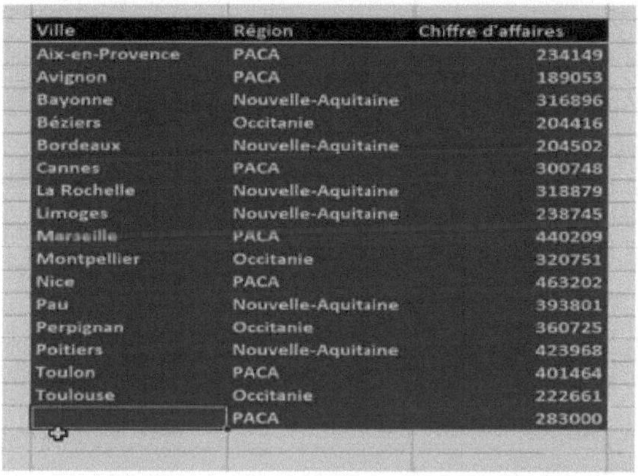

Ville	Région	Chiffre d'affaires
Aix-en-Provence	PACA	234149
Avignon	PACA	189053
Bayonne	Nouvelle-Aquitaine	316896
Béziers	Occitanie	204416
Bordeaux	Nouvelle-Aquitaine	204502
Cannes	PACA	300748
La Rochelle	Nouvelle-Aquitaine	318879
Limoges	Nouvelle-Aquitaine	238745
Marseille	PACA	440209
Montpellier	Occitanie	320751
Nice	PACA	463202
Pau	Nouvelle-Aquitaine	393801
Perpignan	Occitanie	360725
Poitiers	Nouvelle-Aquitaine	423968
Toulon	PACA	401464
Toulouse	Occitanie	222661
	PACA	283000

• If your table has one or more completely empty rows right in the middle (*see illustration below*), Excel may not have taken into account the non-empty rows just after: it has only sorted part of your data. If this is the case, select the whole table yourself using the mouse or keyboard, then run a customised sort (*see multi-column sort below*) to specify the sort criteria more easily.

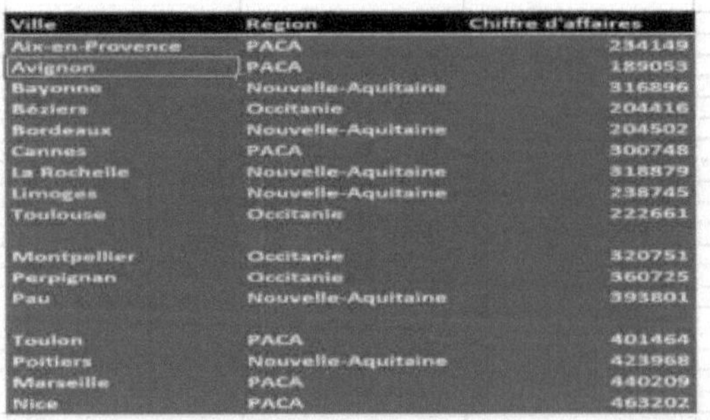

Ville	Région	Chiffre d'affaires
Aix-en-Provence	PACA	234149
Avignon	PACA	189053
Bayonne	Nouvelle-Aquitaine	316896
Béziers	Occitanie	204416
Bordeaux	Nouvelle-Aquitaine	204502
Cannes	PACA	300748
La Rochelle	Nouvelle-Aquitaine	318879
Limoges	Nouvelle-Aquitaine	238745
Toulouse	Occitanie	222661
Montpellier	Occitanie	320751
Perpignan	Occitanie	360725
Pau	Nouvelle-Aquitaine	393801
Toulon	PACA	401464
Poitiers	Nouvelle-Aquitaine	423968
Marseille	PACA	440209
Nice	PACA	463202

. To solve other sorting problems, please also refer to our different sections, which all offer tips depending on the type of data to be sorted.

VIII.4.2.2.SORTING A TABLE WITH SEVERAL COLUMNS IN EXCEL

Sorting a table on several columns at the same time (up to 64!) means sorting it according to several textual and/or numerical criteria, the order of which you specify. It is preferable for the first line of your table to contain column headings, although this is not compulsory.

Before launching a sort, you can either select a single cell in the data range and let Excel select the whole table, which is obviously easier, or select the whole table yourself, including the header row, before launching the custom sort.

First, let's take a quick look at the four methods for displaying the custom sort window.

. **Method 1 -** Click on any single cell in the table, then on the **Home** tab> **Sort and Filter > Custom Sort**.

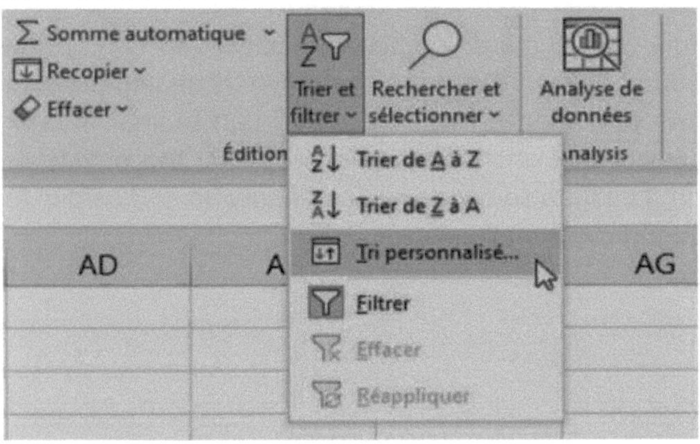

. **Method 2 -** Right-click on any single cell in the table and select **Sort**

> Custom Sort.

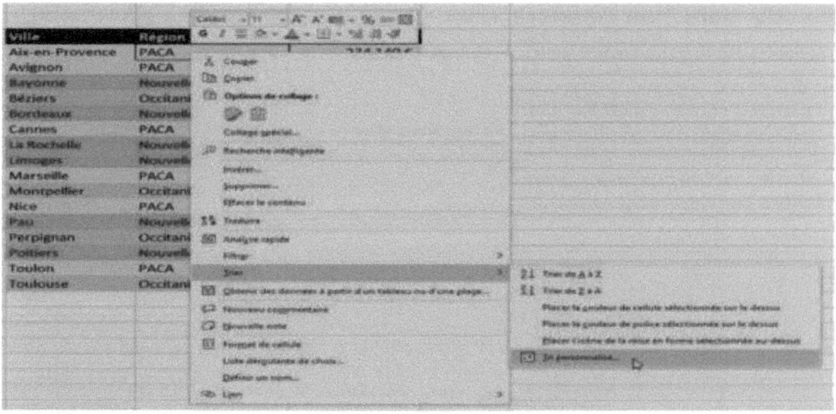

. **Method 3 -** Click on any single cell in the table which, then on the **Data > Sort** tab.

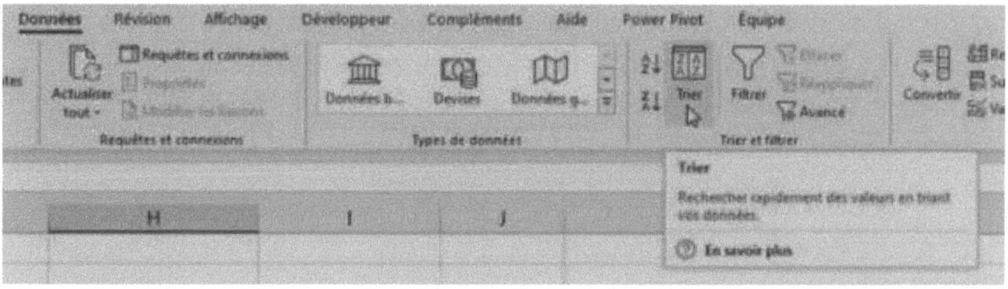

. **Method 4 -** If you have enabled filters for your table, for example via the **Home > Sort and filter > Filter** tab, click on a filter button in the header row and choose **Sort > Sort by colour > Custom sort,** even if you don't want to sort by colour.

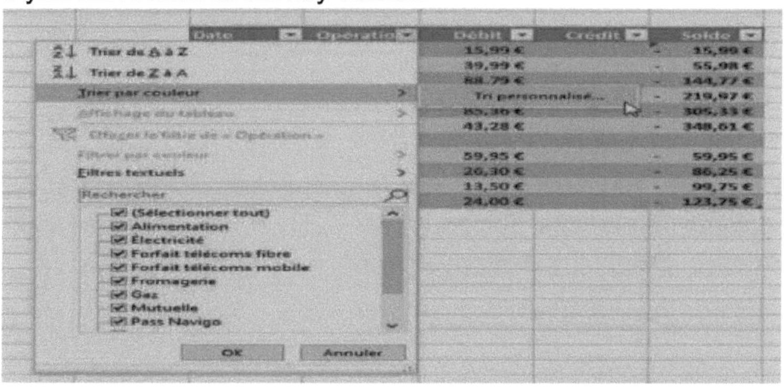

• Whichever method you choose, the **Sort** window appears... Excel selects the whole table and if it detects that the first row of your cell range contains headers (below *City, Region, Turnover*), it ticks the box **My data has headers**. Tick or untick this box if it has made a mistake or if you have selected your cell range yourself.

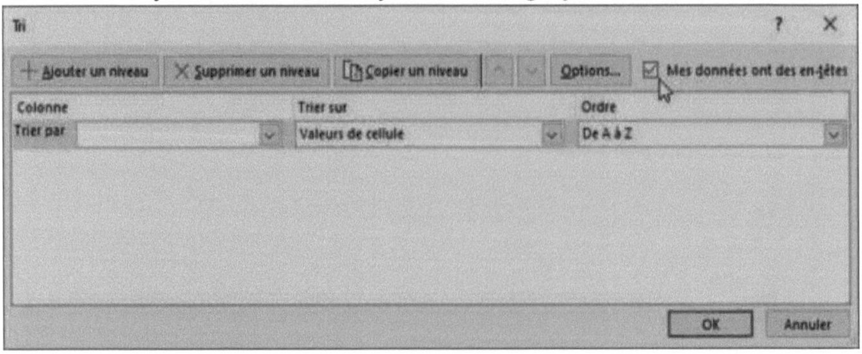

. Specify the first sort criterion. If your data includes a header row, the *Sort by* list shows the titles of your columns. Indicate in the list which column should be used for the first level of sorting.

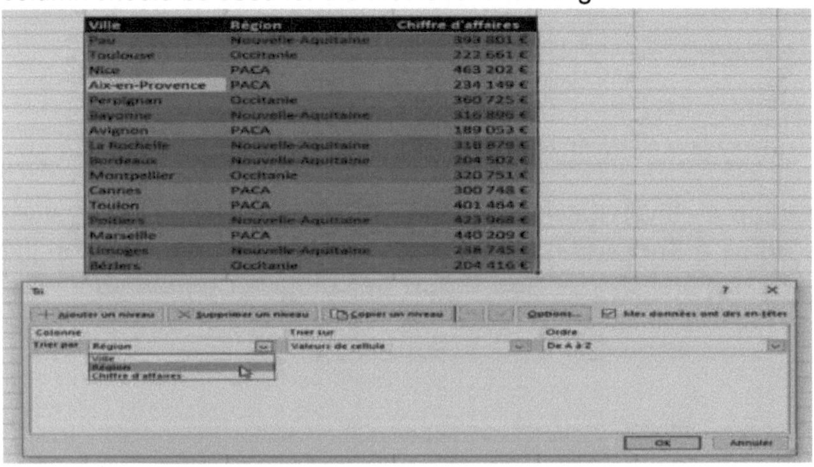

• If the **My data has headings** box is unchecked, Excel will show you the column references, for example C, D, E, etc. This is much less informative! Select the relevant column.

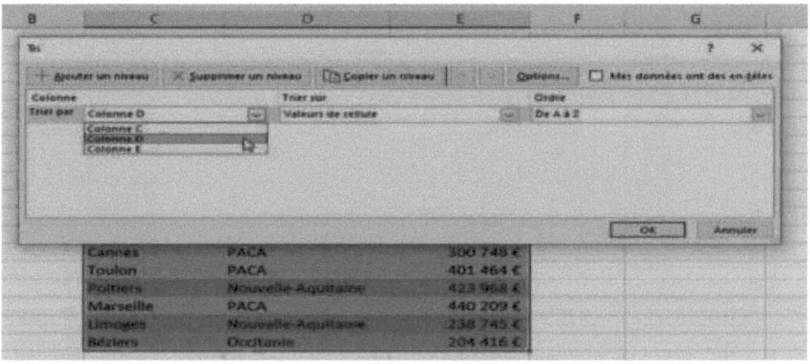

• Whether your data contains text or numeric values such as numbers, dates or times, in the *Sort on* list, leave **Cell values**.

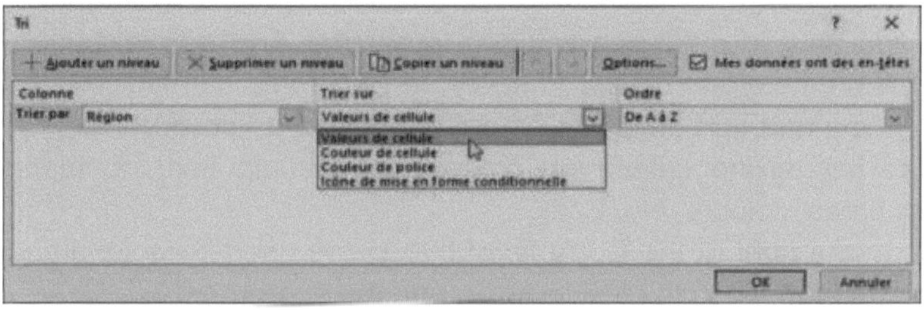

• For this first level of criteria, specify the ascending or descending order: **from A to Z** or **from Z to A** if the column contains text; **from the smallest to the largest** or **from the largest to the smallest** if it contains numbers or times; **from the oldest to the most recent** or **from the most recent to the oldest** if it contains dates.

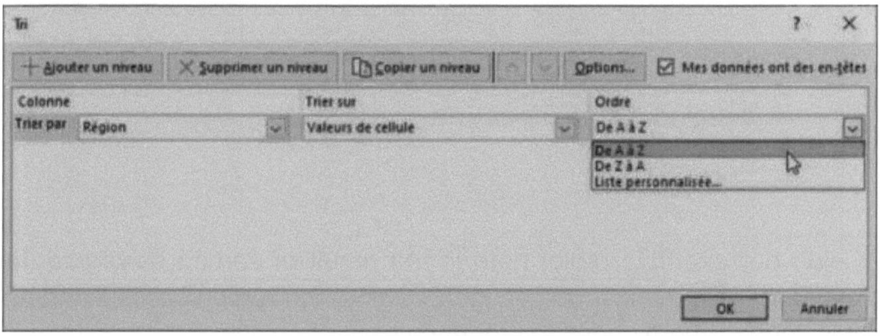

• If your columns contain text, using the **Options** button, you can also ask Excel to differentiate between upper and lower case by ticking the Case **sensitive** box. For an ascending sort, a word in lower case will appear before the same word in upper case, and a word without accents will appear before the same word with accents. In practical terms, after a case-sensitive ascending sort, you get: August, AUGUST, AUGUST, AUGUST, in that order.

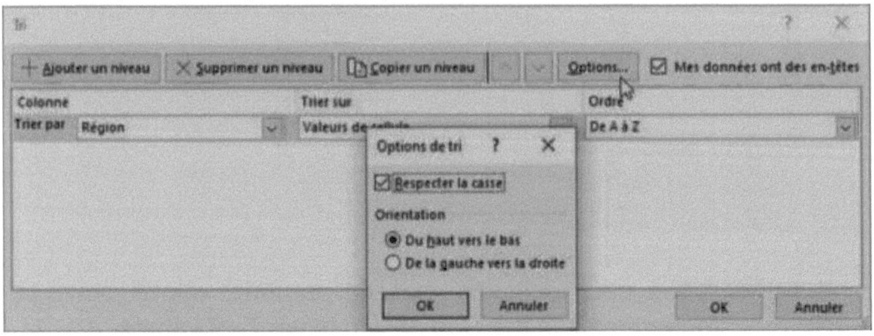

• To add an additional sort criterion, press the **Add a level** button. Excel will create a line below, *Then by*, in which you can indicate the column, type and sort order, as before. You can add several levels in this way, by mixing criteria on columns containing text, numbers, dates or times, colours, etc. Both
buttons to the right of the **Copy level** button are used to move a sort criterion up or down in the list, or to change the sort order.
The highest criteria in the list are sorted before the lowest criteria.
below.

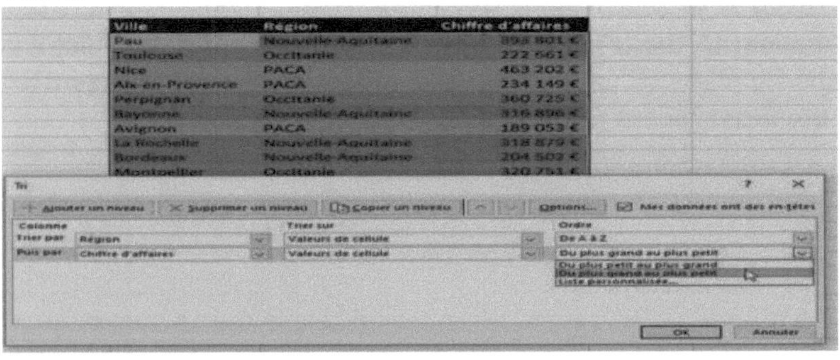

. Using our example table, here is the result of sorting by region (in ascending alphabetical order), then within each region by descending sales figures (the highest first for each region)...

Ville	Région	Chiffre d'affaires
Poitiers	Nouvelle-Aquitaine	423 968 €
Pau	Nouvelle-Aquitaine	393 801 €
La Rochelle	Nouvelle-Aquitaine	318 879 €
Bayonne	Nouvelle-Aquitaine	316 896 €
Limoges	Nouvelle-Aquitaine	238 745 €
Bordeaux	Nouvelle-Aquitaine	204 502 €
Perpignan	Occitanie	360 725 €
Montpellier	Occitanie	320 751 €
Toulouse	Occitanie	222 661 €
Béziers	Occitanie	204 416 €
Nice	PACA	463 202 €
Marseille	PACA	440 209 €
Toulon	PACA	401 464 €
Cannes	PACA	300 748 €
Aix-en-Provence	PACA	234 149 €
Avignon	PACA	189 053 €

- Here's a tip: you don't necessarily need to go through the customised sorting window to sort on two criteria, for example: run a quick sort on your **second** criterion, then run a quick sort on your **first** criterion, and that's it!

. Here's an example Below, to obtain the best turnover rankings for each region (*table on the right*), starting from the initial table (*table on the left*), we first sort on the *Turnover* column, with the best results first; then we sort on the *Region* column from A to Z: the table is sorted. Below you'll find a reminder of the criteria used if you want to obtain the same result using the customised sorting window: this time, first the criterion by region from A to Z, then the criterion by turnover, from largest to smallest.

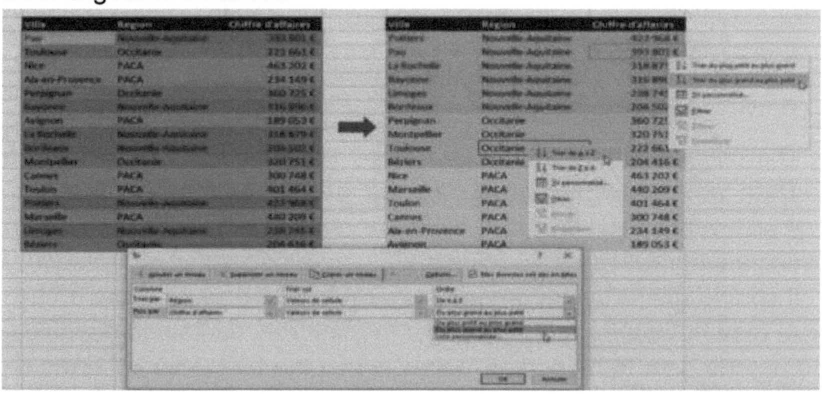

. If the sort doesn't give the results you expected, cancel it (**Ctrl+Z** on PC or **Cmd+Z** on Mac) and refer to our explanations in our other sections, including Converting a column of text into numbers, dates or times and Cleansing data before sorting.

- **III.4.2.3.SORTING TEXT ALPHABETICALLY IN EXCEL**

Do you want to sort your table according to the content of a column containing text or keywords? If you want to sort by ascending or descending alphabetical order, use the method below.

If you want to sort labels that are not relevant to sorting in alphabetical order (days of the week, names of months, a customised list such as TV channels: TF1, France 2, France 3, Canal+, Arte...), please refer to our explanations for sorting according to a customised list.

- Click on **a single cell** in your text column, regardless of the cell. For example, click on a cell in the *City* column to sort the communes alphabetically. Under the **Home** tab, click on **Sort and Filter > Sort from A to Z** to obtain an ascending order, or on **Sort from Z to A** for a descending order.

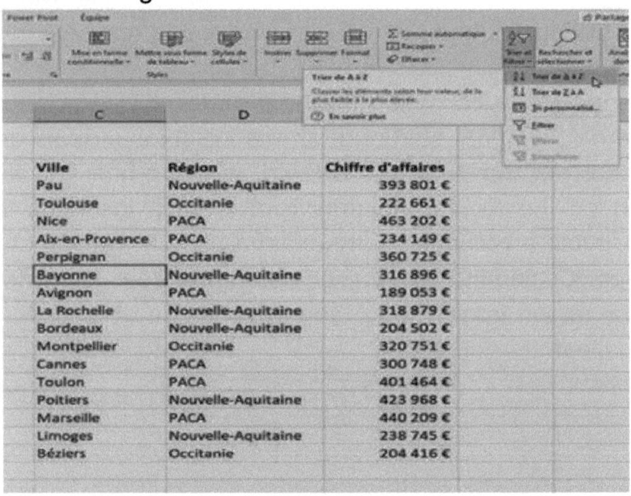

- The other sorting methods described above are equally valid: via the **Data** tab; via a right mouse click; via the filter buttons.
- If you want to sort the table by two or more criteria, see our section Sorting a table with several columns.
- If sorting doesn't work properly in a table with only columns of text, Excel may not have understood that the first row contained headings, and not the data to be sorted. Below, when the first table is sorted on the first names, you can see in the second table that the *Person* and *Day* labels are, alas, sorted like the other data. But if you add, for example, a **bold** attribute to these headings as in the third table, Excel understands their status as headings and does not sort them. Another solution for forcing column headings to be taken into account or not is

to run a custom sort (multi-criteria on several columns), as we saw above.

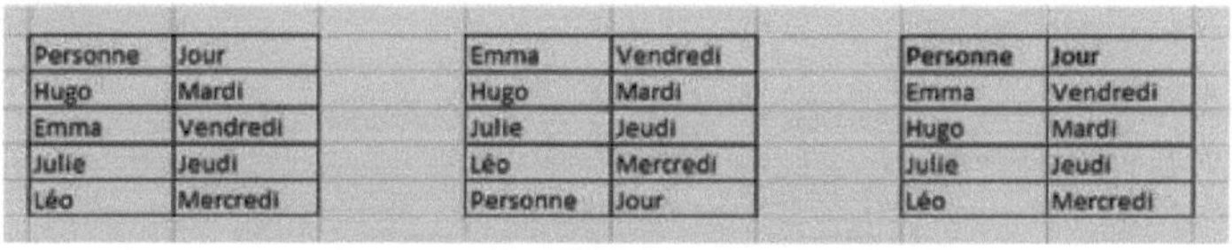

Personne	Jour
Hugo	Mardi
Emma	Vendredi
Julie	Jeudi
Léo	Mercredi

Emma	Vendredi
Hugo	Mardi
Julie	Jeudi
Léo	Mercredi
Personne	Jour

Personne	Jour
Emma	Vendredi
Hugo	Mardi
Julie	Jeudi
Léo	Mercredi

VIII.4.2.4. SORTING NUMBERS IN EXCEL

You can choose between the Home tab, the Data tab, or the context menu that appears when you right-click on a cell...

- Select a single cell, any cell, in the column of numbers that you are using as a sorting criterion.
- Under the **Home** tab, for example, click on **Sort and filter > Sort smallest to largest** (ascending order) or **Sort and filter > Sort largest to smallest** (descending order).

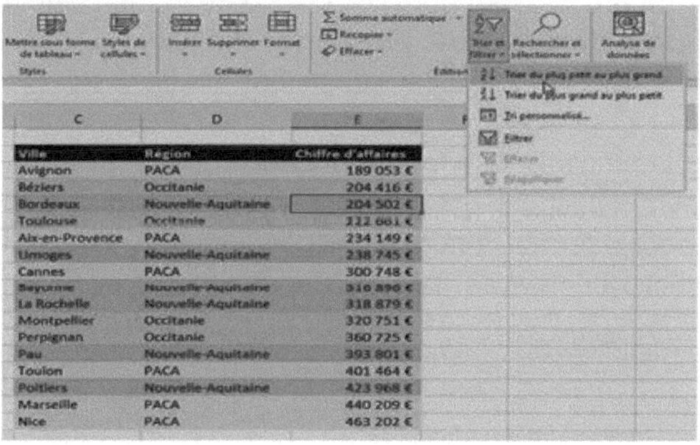

. If sorting does not produce the expected results, some of the numerical data is probably stored as text.

VIII.4.2.5.SORTING DATES IN EXCEL

As you may know, Excel stores dates in the form of serial numbers - whole numbers - to make calculations and sorting easier. As 1st January 1900 is the oldest date that the spreadsheet can handle, this date is given the serial number 1. And 1st January 2021, for example, corresponds to serial number 44197, i.e. the number of days since 01/01/1900. It then doesn't matter what date format you apply to a cell (1/1, 01/01, 01/01/2021, Friday 1 January 2021, etc.), the serial number is the deciding factor. If you want to sort by months or days of the week, go directly to the next section.

. To sort a table by a column of dates, select any one of the dates by clicking on it.

• In the **Data** tab, for example, click on the **A to Z** icon to sort from oldest to most recent, or on the **Z to A** icon to display the most recent dates at the top of the table.

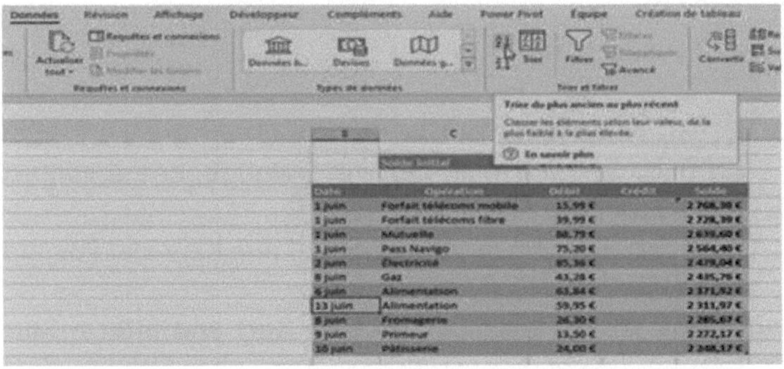

. To sort the table, you can also go to the **Home > Sort and filter > Sort oldest to most recent** tab, or right-click on a date in the column and choose **Sort > Sort oldest to most recent**, for example.

• If sorting by date doesn't produce consistent results, try the following methods...

. Start by displaying a complete date format, including the year if this is not already the case: select the date column, right-click on it, **Cell Format > Date** category, format **14/03/12** or ***14/03/2012**. This will make it easier to check your sorted data and spot any errors in the years entered.

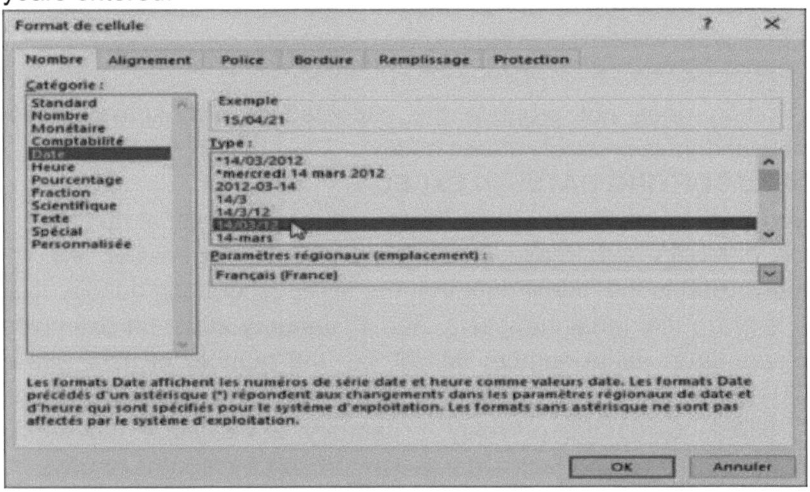

• Another possible cause: some of the dates in the column may be interpreted as text rather than serial numbers.

Worth knowing: Excel for Windows and the versions of Excel for Mac 2016 and 2011 take 1st January 1900 as their starting point. In **Preferences/Options** on Mac and PC, you can also switch to the 1904 date system.

VIII.4.2.6. SORTING MONTHS OR DAYS OF THE WEEK IN EXCEL

If you have typed the names of the months (January, February, etc.) in your column to be sorted, for Excel, as it is text, it will sort these months in alphabetical order: August, April, December, February, etc., which obviously makes no sense. Which obviously makes no sense! Similarly, if Excel sorts the days of the week in alphabetical order, you get Sunday, Thursday, Monday, Tuesday... Fortunately, the spreadsheet offers a solution.

Here's a tip: you wouldn't have to use these customised lists if your column contained full dates (numeric, serial numbers). Select the date column, right-click on it, choose **Cell format**, **Custom** category. In the *Type* field, type **mmmm** to display only the name of the month (*April*) corresponding to this date, or **mmm** to display only the name of the abbreviated month (*Apr*), or type **ddjj** to display only the name of the day corresponding to this date (*Monday, Tuesday...*) or **ddj** to display only the name of the abbreviated day (*Mon, Tue...*).

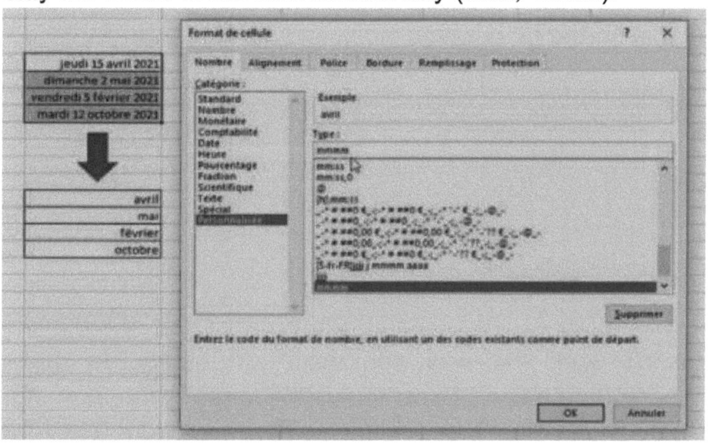

VIII.4.2.7. SORTING HOURS IN EXCEL

Excel displays hours as *05:28:37*, i.e. 5 hours, 28 minutes and 37 seconds. Note that if you just type *05:28* in a cell, it includes 5 hours and 28 minutes, not 5 minutes and 28 seconds. In this case, you should type *0:5:28* or *00:05:28*. Here's how to quickly sort hours of the day (from 00:00:00 to 23:59:59) or even durations longer than 24 hours.

. To sort a table on a column containing hours or durations, select one of the hours in the column, in any cell, by clicking on it.

- In the **Data** tab, for example, click on the **A to Z** icon to sort from the smallest value to the largest, or on the **Z to A** icon to see the most important hours or durations at the top of the table.

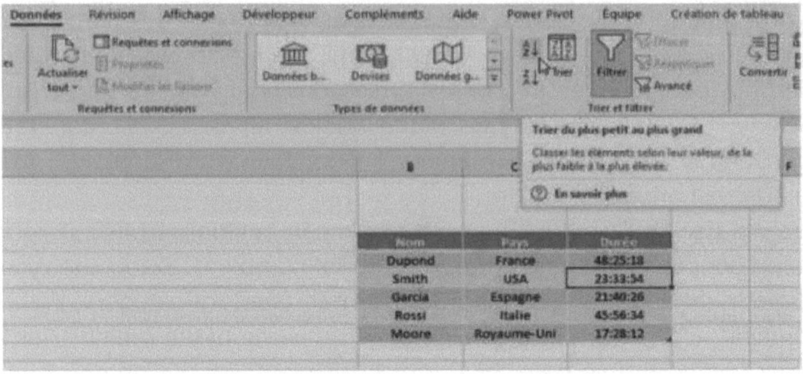

. To sort the table, you can also go to the **Home > Sort and filter > Sort smallest to largest** tab, or right-click on a date in the column and choose **Sort > Sort smallest to largest**, for example.

. Here is our table sorted by duration in ascending order.

Nom	Pays	Durée
Moore	Royaume-Uni	17:28:12
Garcia	Espagne	21:40:26
Smith	USA	23:33:54
Rossi	Italie	45:56:34
Dupond	France	48:25:18

. Sorting doesn't work the way you want? In reality, to make calculations and sorting easier, Excel stores the times in the form of a number with a decimal point. This decimal point ranges from 0 to 1 for times less than 24 hours, with 0 corresponding to at 00:00:00 and 0.99998843 at 23:59:59.

. For times longer than 24 hours, it adds a number *n* before the decimal point corresponding to *n* times 24 hours, for example 2.10135416666667 for 50:25:57, so the 2 corresponds to 2x24=48 hours, and 0.1013541666667 to 02:25:57. But if you apply a Simple

Time display format to a cell containing 50:25:57, Excel will display 02:25:57! The sorting will work correctly, but the display will mislead you.

. So if your timetable column is likely to contain durations longer than 24 hours, make sure you apply the special duration format here: select the range of cells containing the timetables, right-click on it, choose **Cell Format**, click on the **Custom** category in the left-hand column and type **[hh]:mm:ss;@** in the *Type* input box then press **OK.**

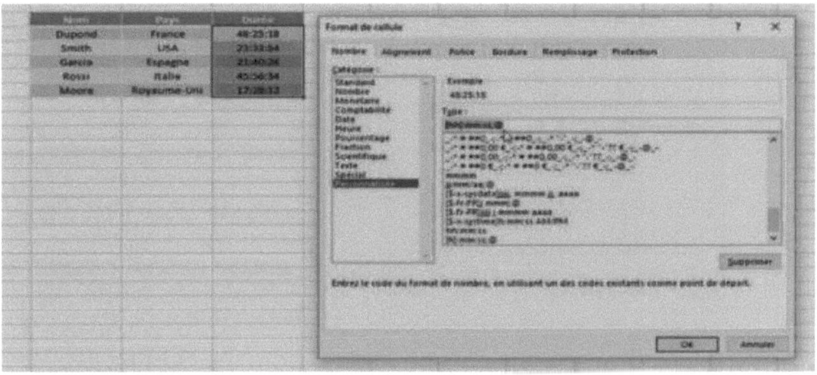

- A little simpler: you can also choose the **Time** category and click on **37:30:55**, which corresponds to a customised display format **[h]:mm:ss;@**

Example: 05:30:27 will be displayed as *5:30:27*, but if you prefer a two-digit display with the zero on the left (so 05 instead of 5), select this format in the **Time** category, then click on the **Custom** category and add an **h** between the square brackets: **[hh]:mm:ss;@.**

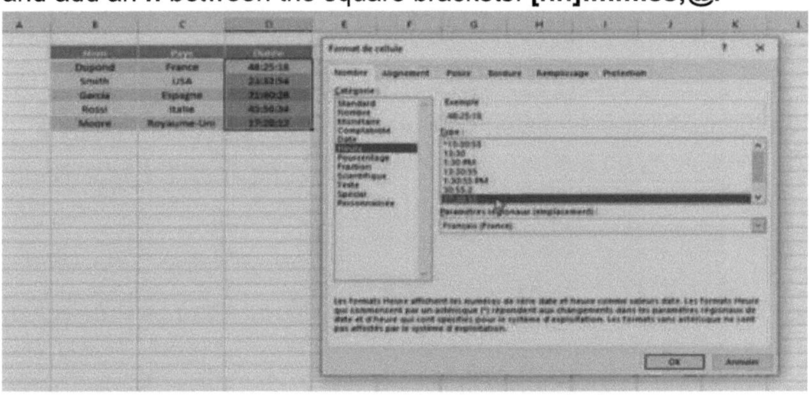

VIII.4.2.8. SORTING BY CELL COLOUR IN EXCEL

If you have applied specific colours to the cells in your table, or if you have asked Excel to apply colours to your data using conditional formatting, the spreadsheet also provides for sorting by cell or font colour. There is no predefined sort order by cell or font colour, so you will have to define the sort order yourself by creating a criterion by colour.

- Select any cell in the table whose elements you have coloured.

. In the **Data** tab, for example, click on the **Sort** button to display the custom sorting window.

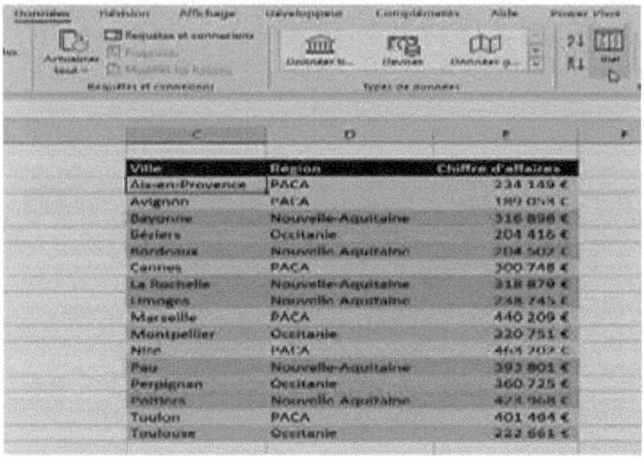

. In the *Sort* window, select a column header from the *Sort by* list. You should always use this same header (in this case *City*) for these colour sort criteria.

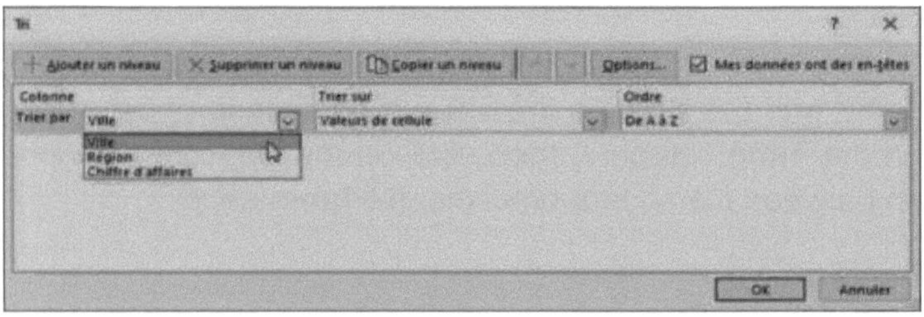

. In the *Sort on* list, select **Cell colour** or **Colour.**
fonts, depending on the formats you have applied to your data.

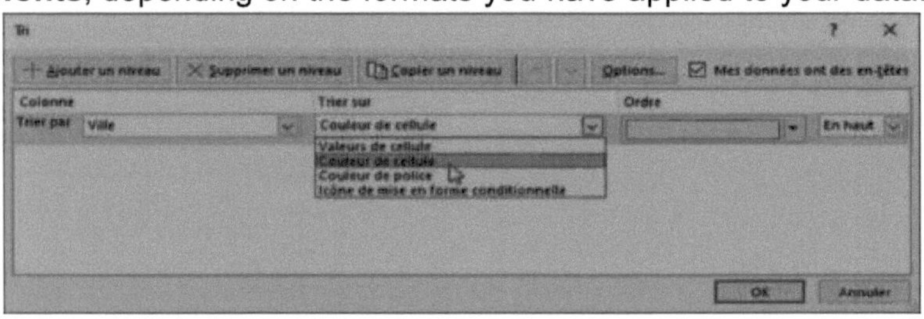

. In the *Order* list, Excel shows you the colours it has detected in the selected column. Click on the colour you want to appear first after sorting and leave **Top** in the list next to it.

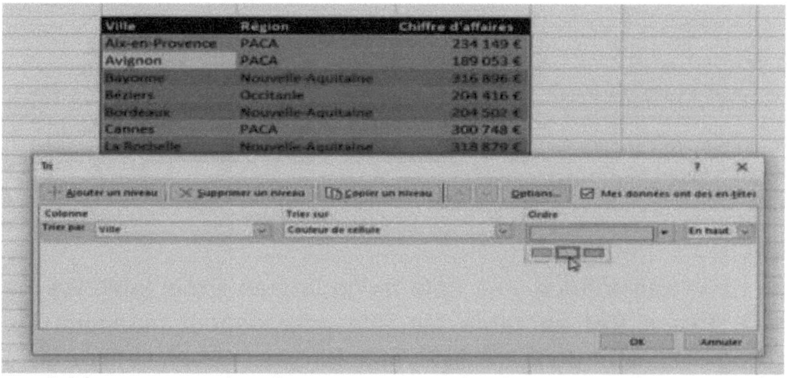

• Add as many levels as you need, always on the same header (here *City*). In the three-colour example below, our third level of sorting is actually superfluous, as the other two colours will appear first anyway. The illustration shows the sorted table.

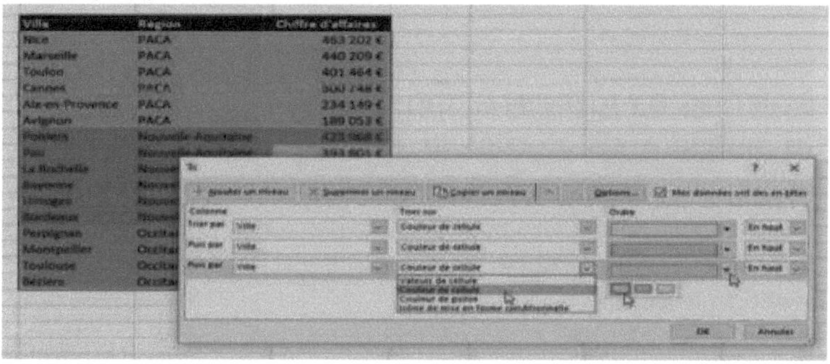

• Right-clicking on a coloured cell in the table with the right mouse button and choosing **Sort > Place selected cell colour on top**. By doing this several times in a row, you can sort the data by colour without going through the custom sort window.

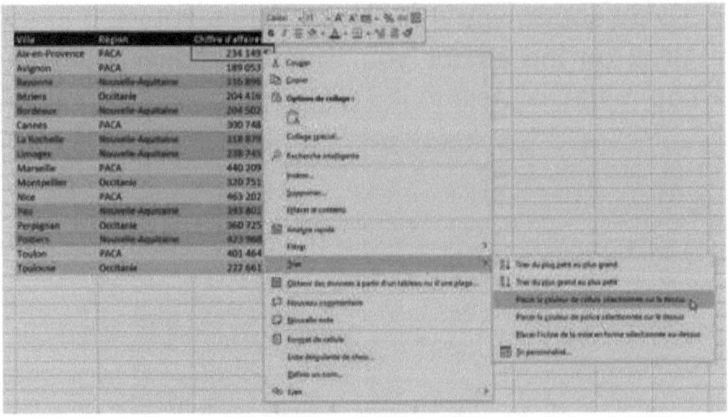

- If you have transformed your data range into an Excel table via the **Home >** Tab **> Set as table** tab, the spreadsheet manages the alternating display of dark and light lines for you. We don't think it's a good idea to sort the data by asking for **the selected cell colour to be placed on top...** But we've tried, and it's possible.

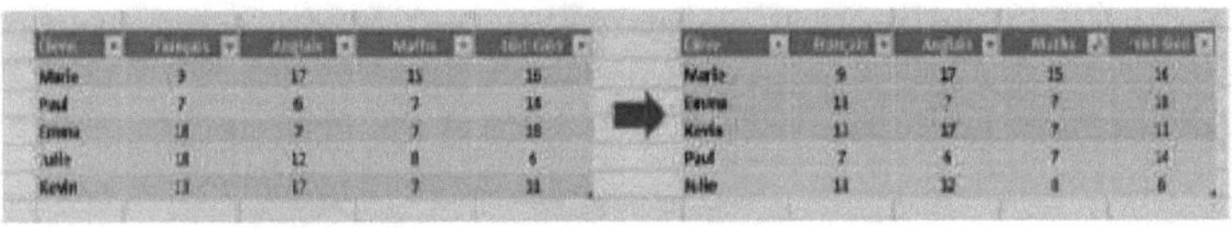

VIII.4.2.9.SORTING BY ICON IN EXCEL

If you have applied a set of icons to your data table using Excel's Conditional Formatting, here's how to sort the data according to the icons.

- Open the custom sort window, for example via the **Data** tab **> Sort and filter** section **> Sort**.
- First select the relevant *Column of* icons, choose **Conditional Formatting Icon** from the *Sort by* list, then select the icon you want to appear first from the **Order** list. Add as many levels as you need.

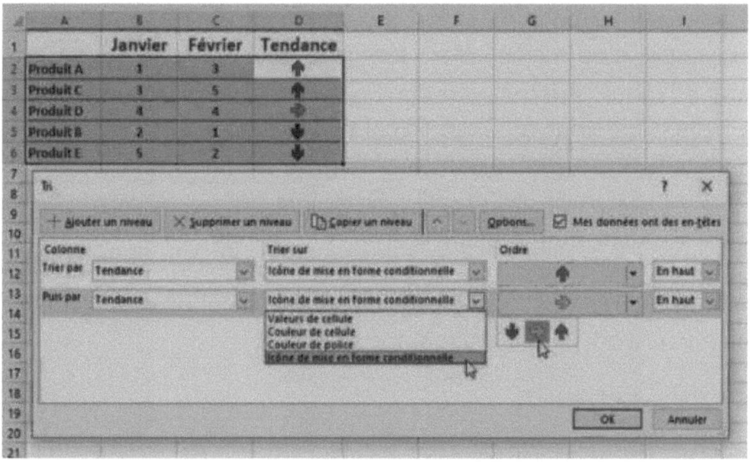

. Another method: in your table, right-click on one of the conditional formatting icons which should appear first, and choose **Sort > Place selected formatting icon on top**.

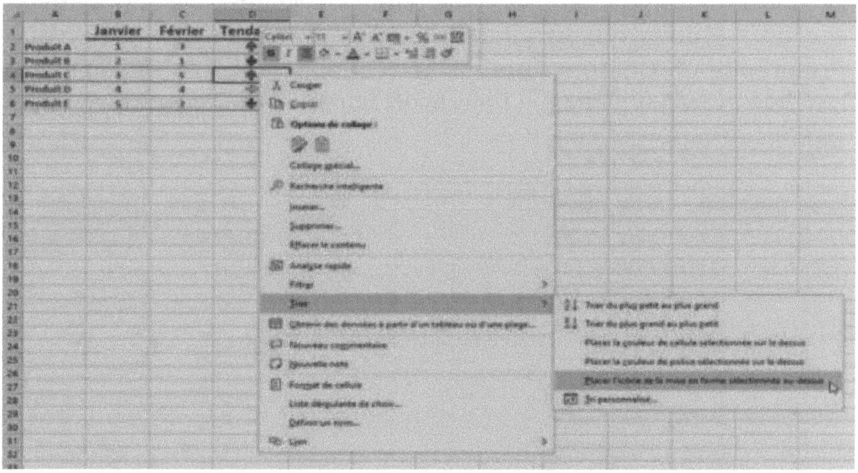

- **III.4.2.10.SORTING WITH A CUSTOMISED LIST IN EXCEL**

The French version of Excel provides you with two customised predefined lists, the names of the days of the week (Monday, Tuesday...) and the names of the months of the year in French (January, February...). You will see here how to use them in a sort. You'll also see how to create other lists with your own labels, which can be used in sorting.

Creating a custom list does two things. Firstly, to define a series of

labels in a specific order for sorting, when it is not appropriate to sort the data alphabetically.
The second advantage is that you don't have to type each name in the list in the cells once you've asked Excel to remember this customised list. For example, type *January* in a cell, grab the little handle in the bottom right-hand corner of the cell... Drag this handle downwards or to the right... Excel automatically fills the range with the other elements stored in the custom list, and in the right order please! This customised list could just as easily be a list of shops or product categories if you work in distribution, for example.

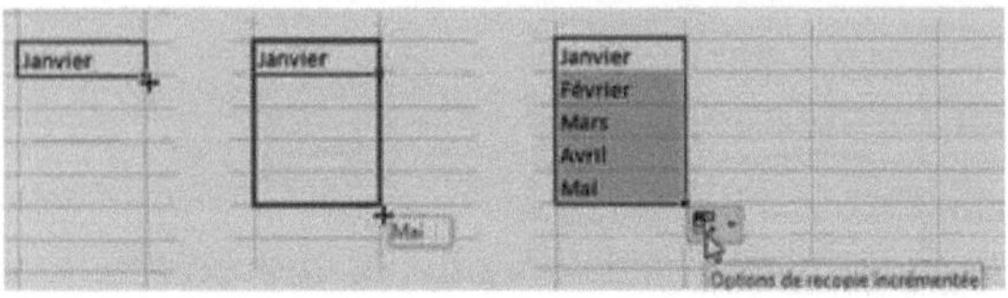

- You can create a custom list on a PC via the **File > Options > Advanced Options** tab (in the left-hand column)**>** in the **General** section **> Modify custom lists** button, or on a Mac via the **Excel > Preferences > Custom lists** menu. (On both Mac and PC, it is also possible to create a custom list directly via the custom sort window, as we will see later).

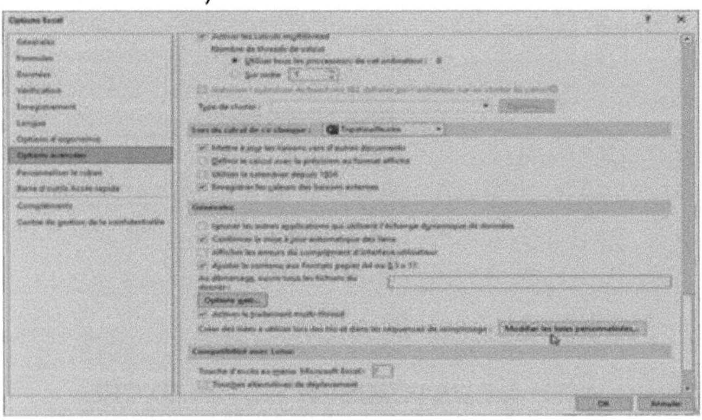

- If your list is already entered in a spreadsheet, select the cell range and press the **Import** button.

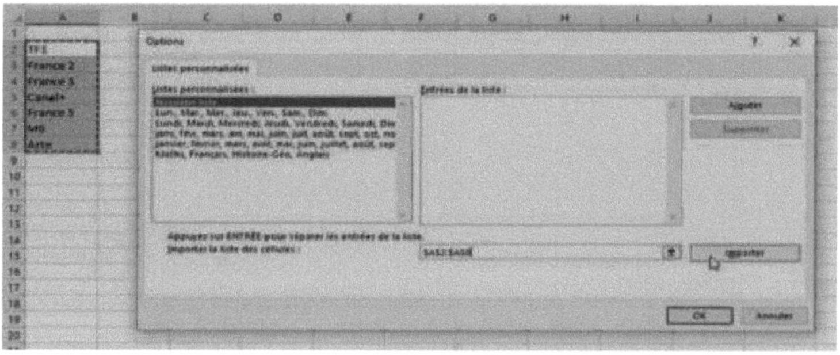

• Alternatively, if it's a small list, you can type it directly into the *List entries* panel. Type the first item, press **Enter**, type the second item, press **Enter** and so on. Type them in the order that makes sense to you. Press **OK** to finish. Below, we create a customised list corresponding to levels of urgency: Critical, Normal, Low.

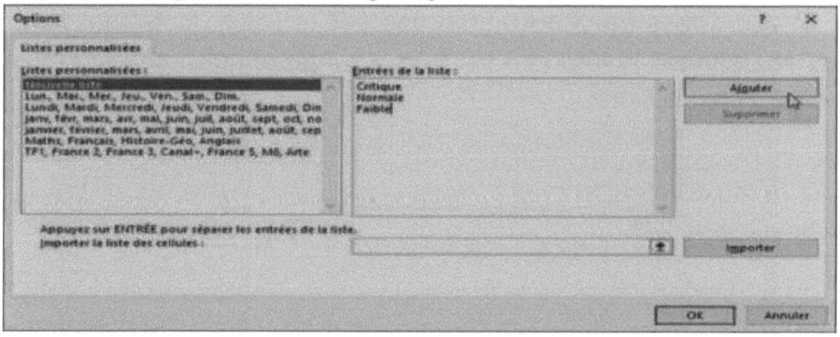

. To sort a range of data according to the values in a custom list, it is preferable that this list already exists (although this is not a requirement). Click on any cell in your table to be sorted.
. In the **Data** tab, for example, click on the **Sort** button to display the customised sorting window.

• Select the *Column* you want to sort by, leave **Cell value** in the *Sort by* list, and in the *Order* list choose **Custom list...**

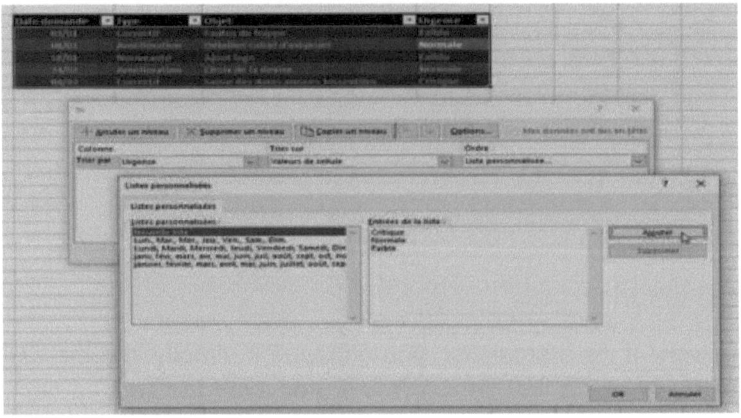

- If your custom list already exists, select it in the left-hand panel. If not, in the *List entries* panel, type in the items in the order that makes sense to you. Press the **Add** button and **OK** to finish. Note that here, you are not allowed to import a list from a range of cells, although this is possible in the options.

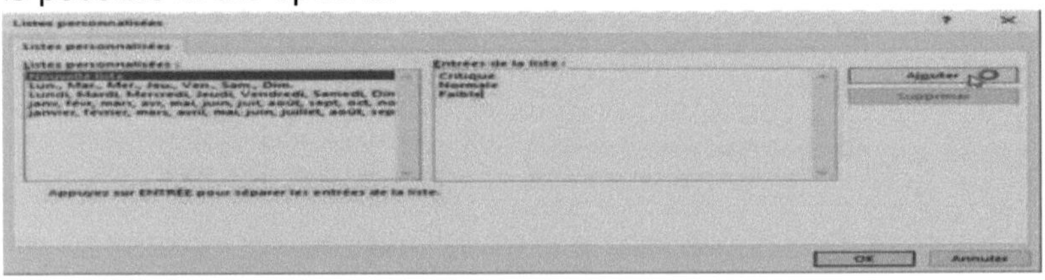

- You can, of course, add other sorting criteria and combine them: below, first the level of urgency, then the date of the request.

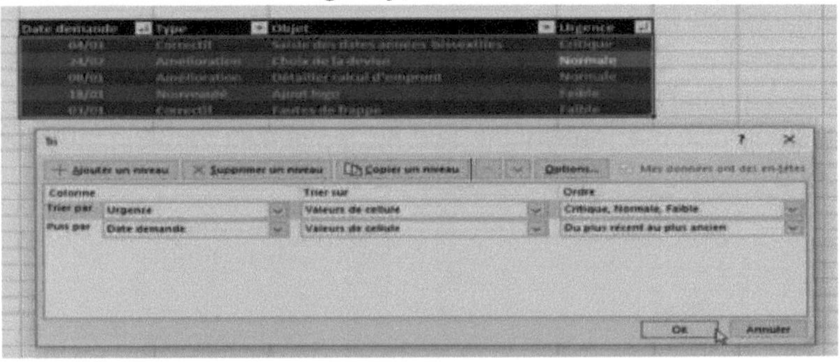

- Would you like to sort by month or day of the week? Click on a cell in the table and choose, for example: **Home** tab **> Sort and filter > Custom sort**.

• Select the name of the column containing the months (or days of the week) and keep sorting on **Cell values**. In the *Order* drop-down list, select **Customised list**. Customised lists of months and days of the week are already provided by Excel, sorted in the correct order, so all you need to do is select one and press the **OK** button. This is the order that will be used to sort your data. Once again, you can combine this sorting criterion with other criteria in other columns.

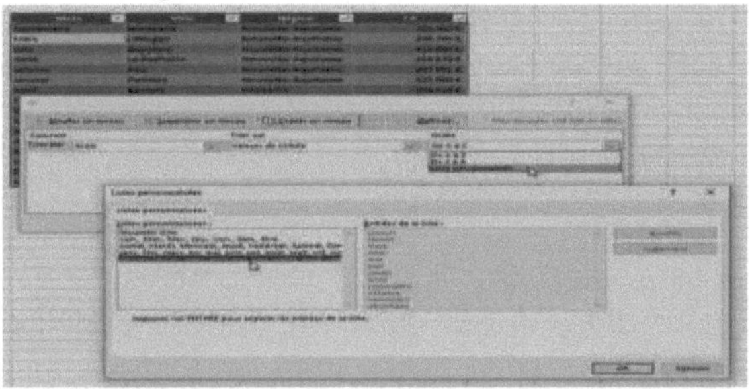

VIII.4.2.11. SORTING FROM LEFT TO RIGHT IN EXCEL

In the vast majority of cases, you will ask Excel to sort your data from top to bottom, row by row. But if you need to sort the data from left to right, so column by column, there's a little option to tick.

This sorting is not possible if you have converted your data range into a table using the **Home > Set as table** tab. You must first cancel the table: click on a cell in the table and, in the **Create table** tab (or **Table** tab on Mac), press the **Convert to range** button.

• Click on any cell in the range of cells to be sorted (Excel will select the whole range), or select the range of cells concerned yourself, as we do below.

• Under the **Data** tab (for example), click **Sort** to display the customised sorting window.

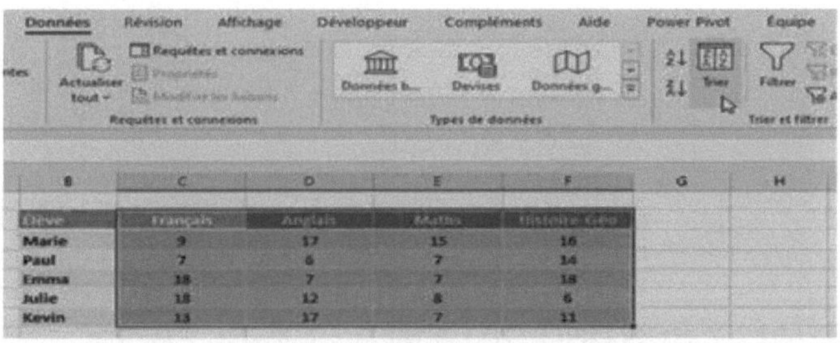

. In the *Sort* window, press the **Options** button. In the small *Sort Options* window, tick the **Left to right** option and press **OK**. If this option is unavailable, your data has been converted into an Excel table.

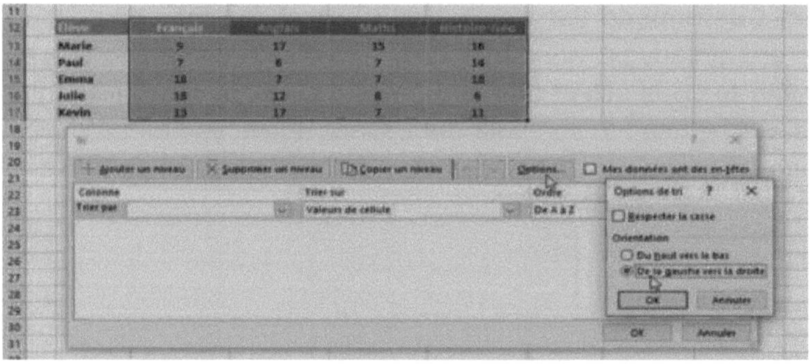

. In the *Line* drop-down list, select the line number containing the labels on which to sort your data, in our case we want to sort the subjects in alphabetical order, so line *12*. We'll keep the **Cell Values** and **A to Z** options provided by Excel, but we could just as easily sort on a custom list.

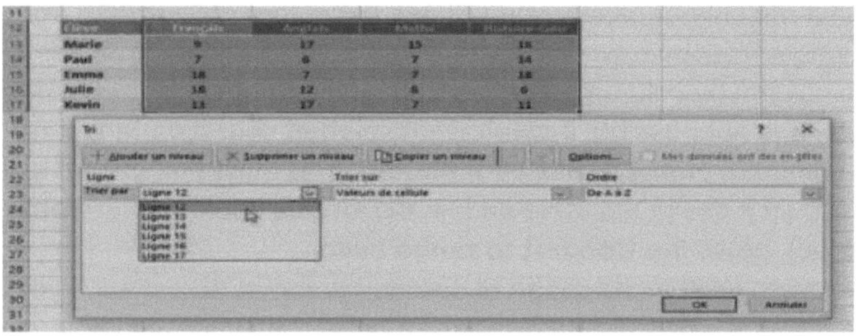

. Here is the table sorted alphabetically by subject. We hadn't selected the *pupil* column, so it hasn't changed after sorting, and each pupil keeps his or her marks.

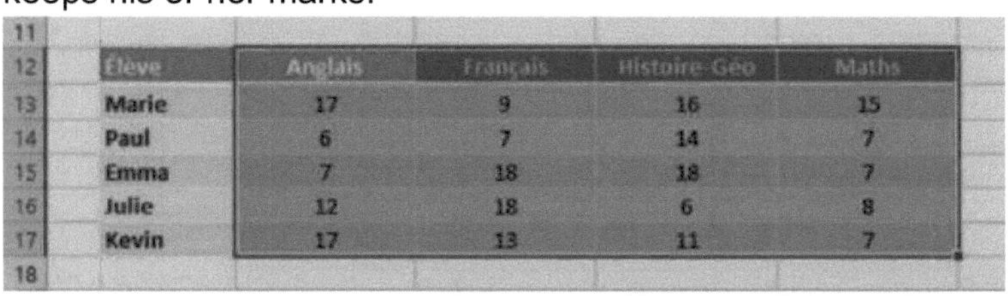

VIII.4.2.12. PARTIALLY SORTING DATA IN AN EXCEL TABLE

Be careful: it is often dangerous to sort only certain parts of a range of data. In the example below, if you sort the selection, Emma will end up with Mary's notes, Mary with Paul's, and Paul with Emma's! But in some cases, partial sorting can be useful...

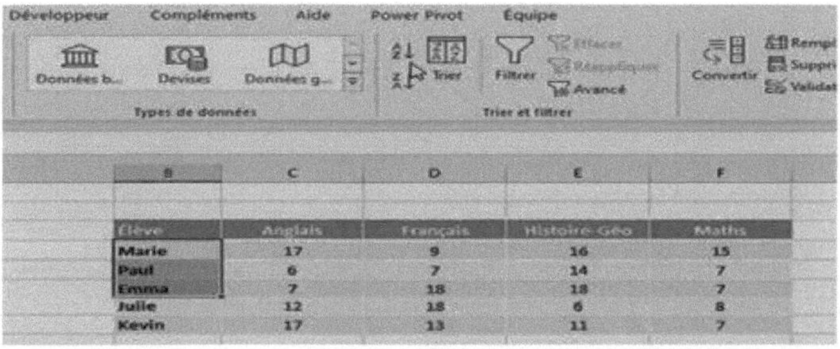

Select the range of cells you want to sort before starting the sort, for example via the **Data > Sort from A to Z** tab.

. If Excel detects that the cells selected are part of a larger whole and that it might be a good idea to select everything, it displays a alert and suggests that you **Extend the selection**. Note that in many cases, Excel will not display this window to extend the selection when it should. So when you launch a sort, select either a single cell or your entire data range, but not any selection of cells thinking that Excel will systematically alert you.

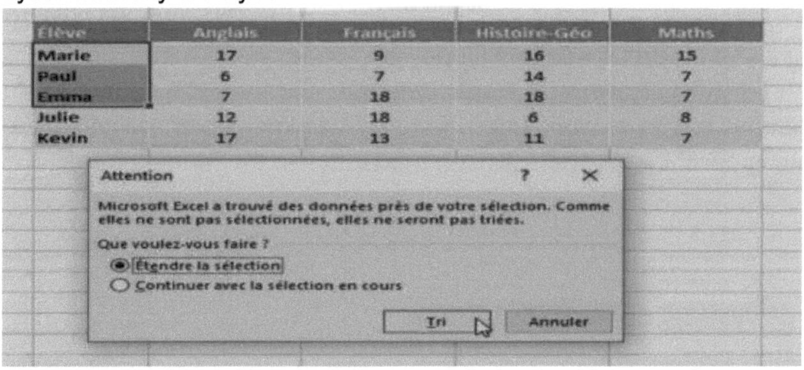

- Note that in an Excel table created via the **Home > Set as table** tab, it is not possible to perform a partial sort on part of the data: Excel sorts the entire table even if you only select part of the data before starting the sort.
- If you find it useful, then select the range of cells and run a quick sort (on the first column) using the **From A to Z** or **From Z to A** icons, or use the **Sort** icon on the **Data** tab to define your own custom sort.

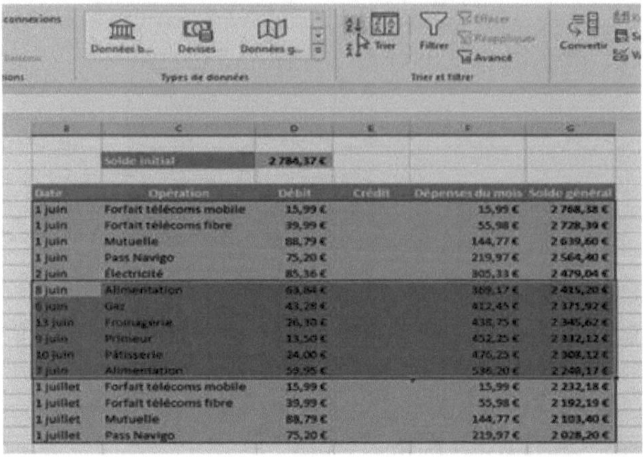

- **III.4.2.13. DYNAMICALLY SORTING DATA IN EXCEL**

Each time your table is modified or supplemented by new rows, you normally have to run a sort again to make sure that your data remains correctly sorted. Unless you ask Excel to sort this data source dynamically! We'll stick here to the dynamic sorting methods offered by recent versions of Excel, which include two functions, **SORT** and **SORTBY**. A tip: it's best to always type function names in lower case; when you press the Enter key, Excel will write them in upper case, at least if you haven't made any typos.

. To sort dynamically on a single criterion, use the **SORT** function. In an empty cell in a worksheet, start by typing**=** ***sort(*** including the opening parenthesis, then click on the **fx** icon in the formula bar.

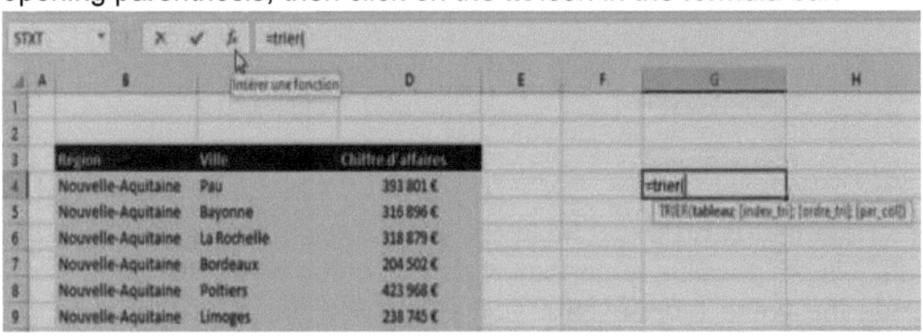

. In the *Function Arguments* window that opens, indicate in the *Table* area the range of cells containing your data, but without the header row. There's no need to type the reference on the keyboard: select the range using the mouse or keyboard, even if it's in another sheet of your Excel file.

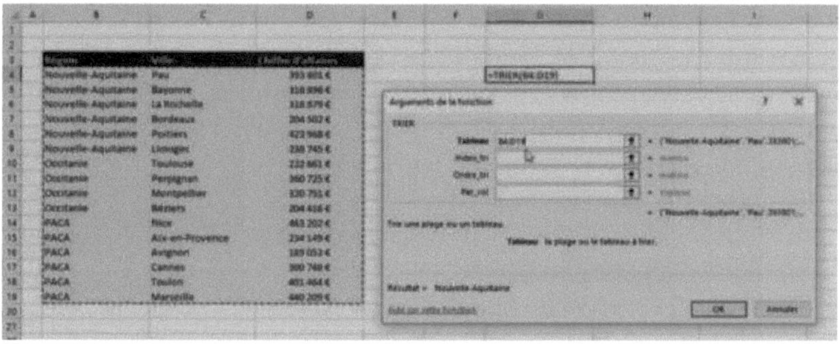

. In the *Sort_Index* field, enter the number of the column containing the sort criterion. In our example it's the third column, *Sales*, that we want to sort, so we type **3**.

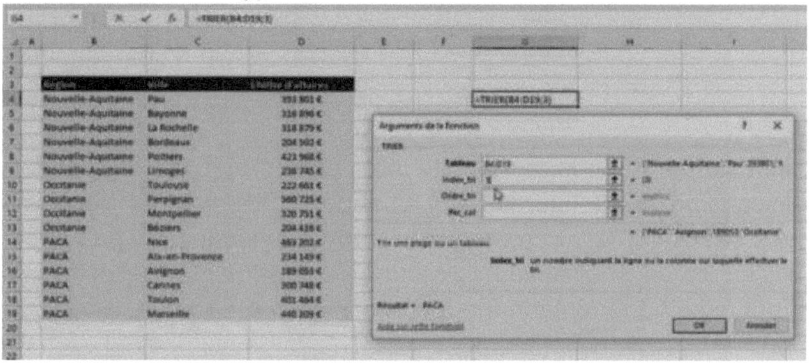

• The last two arguments are optional, you can leave them blank if you accept Excel's default values, the spreadsheet will fill them in for you. In the *Sort_order* field, enter **1** (the default value) for an ascending sort (from A to Z for text, or the smallest numerical values first), and **-1** for a descending sort (the largest values first).

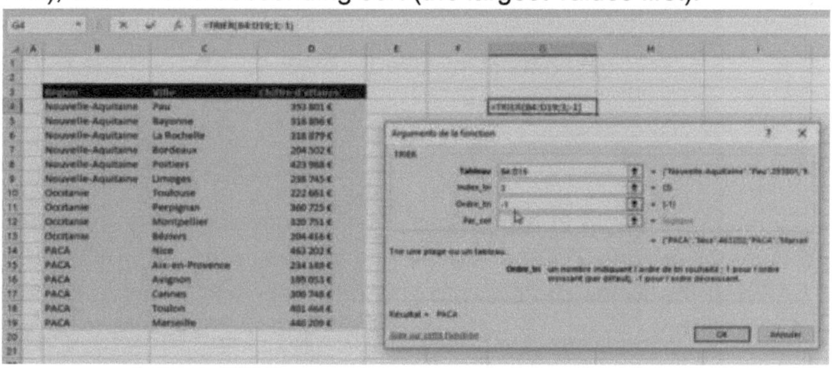

• Leave the *Par_col* field blank to accept its default value. Or enter **false** (default value) for a classic sort by row, and **true** for a sort by column (from left to right). Excel will convert TRUE/FALSE to uppercase if you haven't made any typos.

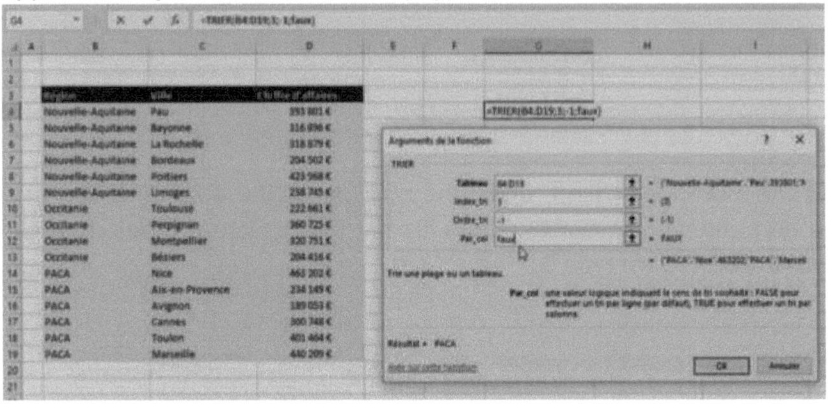

• Here, on the right, is the results table copied by Excel and sorted by descending sales figures. Any change to the original table will trigger a new sort. All you have to do is add the header row and apply formatting. Excel shows you the same formula in all the occupied cells, but only the formula in the top left-hand corner of the range can be modified.

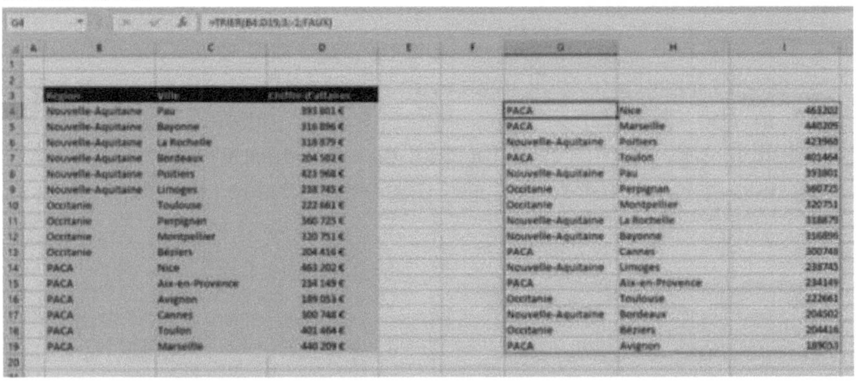

• Type your formula in a part of the sheet with enough empty rows and columns around it. Otherwise, Excel will return an error message *#EPARS!* if the range of cells into which it wishes to "propagate" the data is not empty.

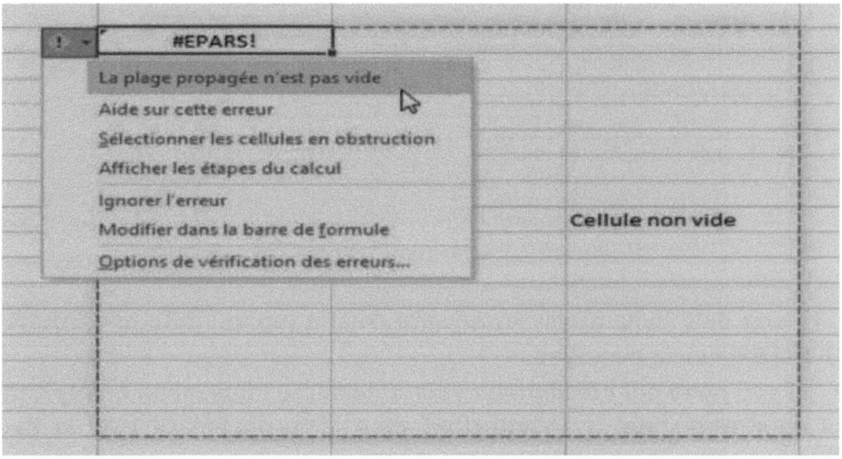

- You can also use the **FILTER** function to select only certain columns from the initial table and/or keep only certain key values. Below, we keep and sort only the towns and their sales, provided that this result is greater than 400,000€.

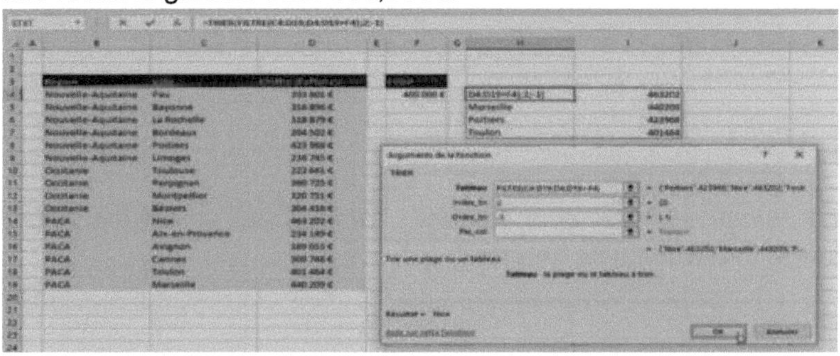

. Here's the result with a reminder of our formula...

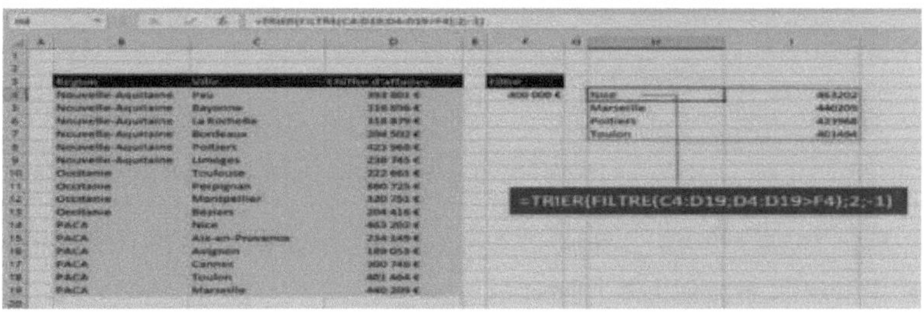

- Refer to this other practical guide to selecting the filter criterion in an Excel drop-down list.

. To sort data dynamically by several criteria (up to 126!), use Excel's **SORTBY** function instead.

- If you have not transformed your data into a table, in an empty part of your worksheet, type **=sortby(** then click on the **fx** icon in the formula bar.

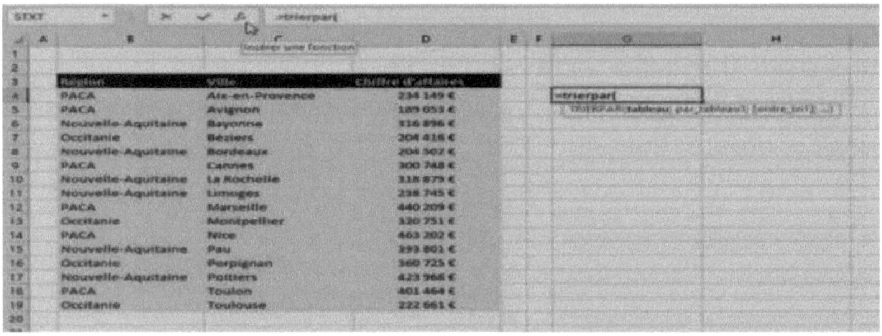

. In the *Function Arguments* window, *Table* zone, select the entire data range, but without its header line.

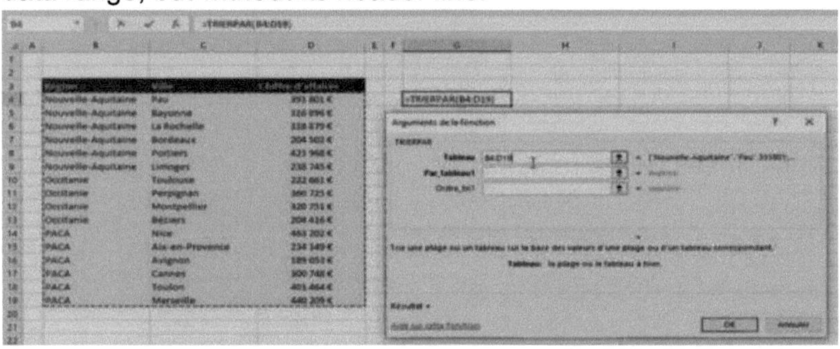

. In the *Par_table1* area, select the column on which to perform the first sort criterion, without its header.

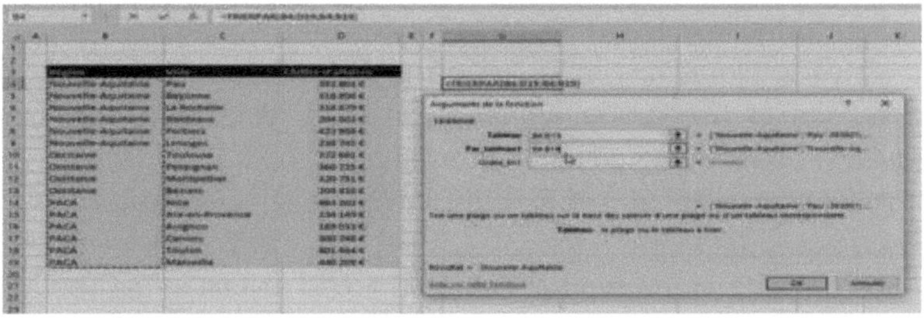

• Leave the *Sort_order1* field blank, or enter **1** if you want to sort in ascending order (this is the default sort order), or enter **-1** if you want to sort in descending order in this column. Fill in the *Par_table2, Ordre_tri2*, etc. fields in the same way, then press **OK**. All the arguments must have the same size, i.e. the same number of cells.

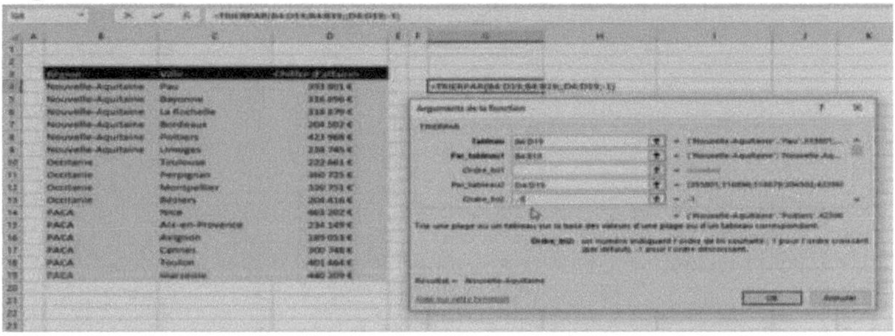

. Here is an example of how we sort our data, in alphabetical order

by region and by declining sales.

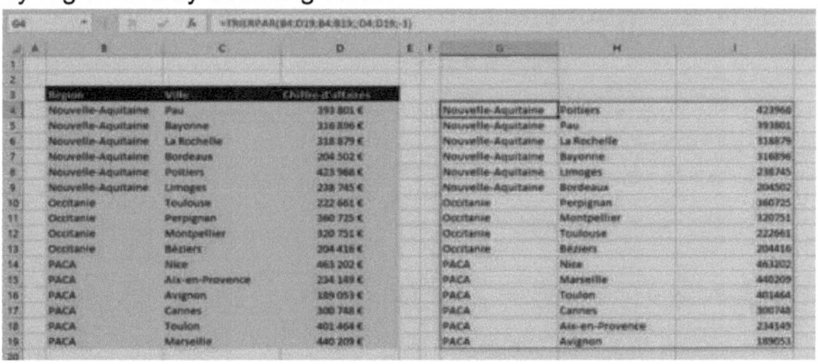

• If you have transformed your data range into an Excel table using the **Home > Set as table** tab, the syntax is slightly different. The first argument to the **TRIERPAR** function will be the name of your table, the arguments *Par_tableau1, Par_tableau2*, etc., will be the name of a header in your table in the form NomDuTablo[NomEn-tete].

. Here is an example with a table we have named *TabRegVilCA*. To sort the regions in ascending alphabetical order and then sort the sales figures in descending order, the formula is :

=TRIERPAR(TabRegVilCA;TabRegVilCA[Region];1;TabRegVilCA[Sales];-1)

• Type this formula in the top left cell, and Excel will fill in the rest of the table!

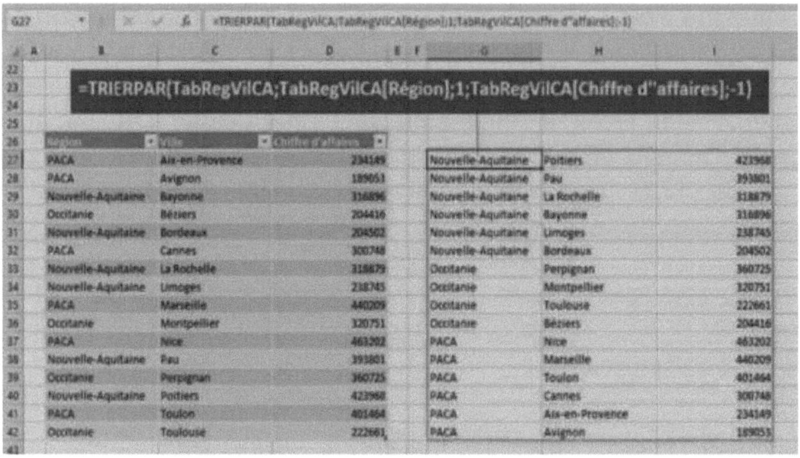

• Note that the **SORT** and **SORTPAR** functions accept different arguments for the sort criteria: **SORT** asks for a column number in the data range, **SORTPAR** asks for a cell range or an Excel table header name.

BIBLIOGRAPHY

❖ **The works**

- Curriculum National des Humanites Techniques Commercials, 2016 ;
- Guillaume PLOUIN, *Cloud computing. Securite, gouvernance du SI hybride et panorama du marché,* 4e edition, Dunod, Paris, 2016.
- Jacques LONCHAMP, introduction aux systemes informatique, Paris, Dunod, 2011;

❖ **Websites:**

- https://www.larousse.fr
- https://www.lalanguefrancaise.com
- www.appvizer.fr
- https://support.microsoft.com
- www.techno-science.net

MIX
Papier aus verantwortungsvollen Quellen
Paper from responsible sources
FSC® C105338

FSC
www.fsc.org

Printed by Books on Demand GmbH, Norderstedt / Germany